Trying to Understand Brazilian Culture

Andrew Creelman

Contents

Chapter One – How I Ended Up In Brazil

My journey to Brazil actually began in rural Japan, where I'd been teaching kids how to speak English for about three years. I loved Japan, the people, the culture and the food; I'd even become indifferent to 'Hello Kitty'. But then, one night in my local bar, I had a conversation with my Japanese friend Kazu that inspired me to shake things up a little. It was a conversation that went something like this:

"I finish university in three months," he began. "I think I will travel for three weeks before I start working." I thoughtfully took a mouthful of beer and then asked him where he planned to go.

"Brazil," he said without a moment's hesitation. "I want to go to Brazil during Carnival and then travel around the country."

"That sounds amazing. I'd love to go there," I sighed dramatically, with the type of sincerity that didn't seem all that excessive after a few beers.

"So, come with me!"

"I can't. I have my job here and they will never give me three weeks off work."

"But, Andrew, you're always telling me how much you don't like your job."

He was right; I was *that* fun sponge who would soak the enjoyment out of our Thursday night drinking sessions by talking about how much I didn't enjoy teaching these kids. In my defence, though, my lunchtime class with the dreaded Tamaki the next day would always play heavily on my mind. This two-and-a-half-year-old girl would literally scream her way through our 30-minute class each week. Standing there with a set of puppets on each hand (otherwise known as Kim the Kangaroo and Ali the Antelope) in the hope I could win the attention of this miserable little child really bothered me. Her pushy mother always ignored how piercingly loud Tamaki's screams were during these classes too, and was indifferent to seeing the tears of sadness rolling over her daughter's chubby little cheeks.

I felt more like I was implicit in Tamaki's torture than I was her English teacher.

I was also confused by who got the most out of our English classes as it wasn't Tamaki who'd throw herself into each element of them with passion, but her mother. Sometimes Tamaki would be left slumped up against the wall crying, as me and her 30-something-year-old mother would follow the instructions on the CD by jumping around like a kangaroo, swinging our arms like a monkey in time to the music or dancing to the 'ABC song'. There was never any doubting Tamaki's mother's commitment to class. Tamaki, however, clearly longed to be anywhere but in that room with us.

 "Why don't you just quit your job and come to Brazil with me for Carnival?" asked Kazu.

I instantly knew this was a great idea and I told him so. I was done with dancing to 'The Weather Song' like a failed kid's TV presenter and I was done with miming the 'Days of the Week Song' to children who resented me for taking their crayons away from them. I was also done with the stinking puppets I brought to life every class. The next day I went into work and immediately handed in my three-month notice.

Kazu and I in Japan, a few weeks before leaving for Brazil

I'd love to say my boss was distraught when I told her, that she collapsed into a heap on the floor, grabbed at my legs and pleaded with me to stay because I was such a valued member of staff. She really didn't. "I'll start looking for a new teacher then," she announced, with about as much emotion as a dental hygienist talking about the weather. There was no backing out now!

A few days later I met Kazu again to discuss where in Brazil we wanted to travel to. He understandably wanted reassurance that I'd definitely quit my job, because handing in your notice with so little thought wasn't the sort of thing Japanese people did. But by this point, I was all in.

As we began talking it was clear that outside of Rio and the Amazon we had no idea what else the country had to offer. What we did know was that we planned to utilise the time Kazu had available between finishing his university exams and starting his placement in a hospital. As a doctor, he would inevitably be swallowed up in the Japanese hospital system without much in the way of holidays for a while, so these three weeks meant a lot to him. And as if to demonstrate how much, he proved his commitment by pulling a brand new Brazil guidebook from his backpack. I'd tried to get an English version too, but this was asking too much from my local bookshop that offered very few books in English outside of *The Babysitters Club* collection.

As soon as the plastic wrapper had been removed, we sat down and inspected the book's first chapter on Rio. Then he flicked to the next chapter and asked, "What about this place?" I looked at a picture of São Paulo but wasn't impressed by the bland-looking skyscrapers on the page. "Nah," I responded quite flippantly, "I mean, it just looks like any other city, doesn't it? Why the hell would we want to go to São Paulo?"

No sooner had I asked this than he was taking a second look at the picture for himself. "You're right," he conceded, "but I think that a trip to the Japanese district of São Paulo would have been interesting. It says here that the city has the largest settlement of Japanese people living outside of Japan."

"Kazu, we live in Japan right now," I argued. "I don't want to fly halfway around the world to sit and eat sushi in a bar run by Japanese people. We can do that here!"

Catching the dopiness of his idea he laughed, "Yes, you're right!" Within seconds of rejecting going to the city we began looking at the next chapter of the book on the Iguazu Falls. In hindsight the reason we dismissed São Paulo so quickly was because it just wasn't the Brazil we wanted to buy into. When we first thought about visiting the country, it was the beautiful beaches and natural scenery that sprang to mind, not cities cased in concrete. So skipping it on our trip was a total no-brainer for us because we had no great desire to go and see it – not with all the other places of beauty on offer. But on our tight budget we worked out that we'd need to go from Rio to the Iguazu Falls by bus, an incredibly long journey. So we decided to break this trip up with a daylong stop-off in São Paulo.

We booked our flights a few days later and the next few months flew by surprisingly quickly. Before I knew it, the time to take off my Kim the Kangaroo and Ali the Antelope puppets had arrived, and so too had the day I had to say goodbye to Tamaki. She cried when we said goodbye; I really hadn't expected anything less! The thought of not having to hear her screams every week even brought a tear to my eye too!

Just twelve and a half weeks intervened between me quitting my job and arriving in Rio. After landing in the country we cleared immigration, grabbed our backpacks and hurried through to the airport's arrivals lobby. There we were given our first glimpse of Brazil. Waiting for me and Kazu was a pot-bellied taxi driver in an ill-fitting tee-shirt and Hawaiian shorts. We recognised he was there to pick us up because he was fanning this sweat-stained tee-shirt with the board that had our names scribbled across it.

I'm not going to lie to you: this welcome to Brazil was a lot less sexy than I had imagined!

Our six days in the "marvellous city" were spent relaxing on the beaches of Copacabana and Ipanema, enjoying street parties and also visiting sightseeing locations that gave breathtaking views of the city. Neither one of us particularly wanted to move onto São Paulo when our time there drew to a close, yet with Rio surpassing our expectations we were feeling optimistic about what else Brazil had to offer.

Kazu in Santa Teresa, Rio

After a six-hour bus journey we'd made it to São Paulo, navigating our way by metro to Brigadeiro station. It was only as we ascended on to the street by escalator that I began to feel slightly intimidated. In front of us was a sea of skyscrapers that continued down Avenida Paulista as far as the eye could see. We'd booked a hostel just off this street purely because Kazu's guidebook had recommended this avenue as a 'must see', a place you couldn't possibly miss on a trip to São Paulo. But as we looked around I began to question if the reviewer had ever been here. It was just so big and so unapologetically ugly.

By this point Kazu was already unfolding a hand drawn map that would guide us to our hostel. With him busying himself I took a further look at people passing by, most dressed in business attire and armed with umbrellas. The city we were in the midst of definitely seemed to have a different vibe to the one we'd encountered in Rio. It was here my eyes were opened to the reality of what living in Brazil would really be like. Carnival isn't something that happens every day, so our experiences in Rio weren't really the best way to gauge what Brazilian culture was truly about. These umbrella-wielding business people offered a glimpse of a Brazil I'd not really considered before: a Brazil where people went to work!

"OK," Kazu said, nodding at me, "I think I know where we're going."

After a few blocks we turned onto some quieter streets that eventually led to our hostel. We checked in, made our beds and then promptly fell asleep for the rest of the evening. Feeling somewhat refreshed the next day, we went to another place recommended by Kazu's guidebook: Ibirapuera Park. As tranquil as the park seemed it just didn't inspire much in the way of affection from us, perhaps because the beauty of Rio had spoiled us. I felt fairly nonchalant about Ibirapuera, which summed up what I thought about São Paulo during my first 24 hours too. The city seemed huge, fast-paced and chaotic, yet strangely bland and characterless all at the same time. Our day trip had been pleasant, but we were itching to see more natural landscapes. So, with our cameras fully charged and our bodies somewhat recovered, we arrived at the same bus terminal we'd been at the day before to take a sixteen-hour bus journey over to the Falls.

Me, thinking I looked absolutely gorgeous by the Falls

The falls were phenomenal, but as darkness fell on them there wasn't much to do except rest our worn-out feet and use the free Internet in the hotel. This was something I did for a good two hours trying to find a place that would offer us a more interesting take on São Paulo than the one we'd been given. I decided upon a hostel in the bohemian district of Vila Madalena which turned out to be a wise move. On our return we were instantly seduced by the European-style bars and the cosmopolitan atmosphere of the neighbourhood. We'd also returned on a Saturday, so were curious to sample the city's nightclub scene.

The club we ended up in was a lot of fun, and, despite not really understanding how the hell you were supposed to order drinks and then pay for them with the plastic card we'd been given, we danced to some great electronic music until the sun came up.

Second time around São Paulo had made a very different impression on us, and, as we took our taxi to the airport for the last leg of our trip (The Amazon), I remember saying to Kazu that there seemed a lot more to São Paulo than had originally met the eye. On reflection it was at this point a seed was planted inside my head, one that would later grow into full-blown intrigue about how I'd fare in the city on a more permanent basis.

For the next three days, though, we relaxed in a lodge within the Amazon jungle. Every morning a buxom middle-aged Australian woman would appear at breakfast to discuss, in detail, how her upset stomach would prevent her from going on any of the day's excursions. Despite having a very strong grasp of English, Kazu would pretend he couldn't understand a word she was saying so that her diarrhoea woes were directed squarely at me and her long-suffering husband (whose idea of a romantic Amazon break had turned out to be anything but!).

Piranha fishing in the Amazon

Before we knew it we were taking our flights back to Japan with memory cards full of pictures and bank cards that had seen better days. On this flight I had more than enough time to reflect on how much I'd enjoyed our 'once in a lifetime trip'. Yet I was already thinking that 'once' wouldn't be enough for me: I wanted to go back.

As soon as I was in Japan the first thing I needed to do was find myself a new teaching job. After a week of searching online and one successful job interview later, I'd bagged a position as an assistant language teacher in a Japanese high school. What this meant was that I'd be working with kids aged between twelve and thirteen, and would be required to stand in front of the class to read from a text book (when prompted by the English teacher). This was literally the main role of my job! A few days into my first week at the school, the head of English took me to one side and confided something to me. He said that he'd really wanted an American teacher for the position so the kids could learn American English, but, with no American candidates, the school had become desperate and decided to just hire me. He explained that he'd really appreciate it if I could adopt an American accent during classes. I'm really bad at accents, and the best I could do was a pretty shocking Forrest Gump impersonation, which surprisingly pleased him. At first I was amused that I was being paid to talk like this, so I agreed to do my Tom Hanks impression in all of our classes. But a few weeks into hearing kids mimic me I became concerned that I was responsible for their American English drawl. I feared one day they would talk to other native English speakers like this.

Ultimately when talks of re-contracting came about, the job just wasn't fulfilling enough to keep me there for a second year. So, I declined the offer of re-contracting, safe in the knowledge I'd already secured a job in São Paulo. I was going to be working in a call centre selling finance packages to business people. If ever there was a job I'm incredibly unsuited to, this is it! I think I knew it at the time, but I wanted to get back to Brazil with a job … any job!

It was only as I was sat on my flight over there (chewing on my bag of complimentary peanuts and watching the random episode of *Friends* on the screen in front of me) that I began to question if going back was such a good idea. Not really an ideal time to be seriously thinking about this decision, I know! I'd moved to a foreign country before, of course, but I'd done so in the knowledge that there would be someone waiting for me at the other end of my flight to ease me into my new life. I also had a guaranteed salary instead of the commission based one this position offered. Truth be told, I'd accepted the call centre job despite having no interest in finance. I also had no desire to start studying another language from scratch and I knew only one person in São Paulo: a friend-of-a-friend. Despite all of this I was optimistic. I was determined to make the most of this opportunity and I refused to be deterred by something as trivial as moving to a different continent with no real idea of what I was getting myself into!

Looking back, I genuinely don't recognise this carefree earlier self. Failure wasn't something I'd even considered. I feel like I'm writing about someone else right now, a character from a straight-to-DVD film who I'm sat rooting for!

As my flight touched down in São Paulo I felt a mixture of nerves and excitement. I collected my suitcase and walked out of the airport's exit where I was greeted, not by a sweaty taxi driver with a slight case of halitosis, but by huge palm trees towering over me. I saw people walking to the car park with their families, friends and business associates. In contrast, I was standing there on the tarmac cutting a rather solitary and confused-looking figure. "Right," I said aloud to myself, "let's do this." I flagged down a taxi and passed the driver the piece of paper I'd written my new address on. He nodded at it in recognition, quoted me a ridiculous price and then I climbed in. With the door slammed shut he sped off deep into the largest city in Southern America: the place I've come to call home ever since.

Chapter Two – Settling In

You probably won't be surprised to hear that my glittering career in the world of finance didn't last long at all: two months, three weeks and a day and a half to be precise. It had become clear to me very early on that the job wasn't going to be nearly as lucrative as I'd hoped. What I mean by lucrative is that I wasn't actually making any money at all! Each day I'd sit in a windowless room for up to ten hours a day with my English colleagues, where we'd read a script over the phone. This was done in English to Brazilian business executives, many of whom didn't speak the language well enough to understand what the hell I was talking about. I pitched these guys with the intention of persuading them to invest in things like retirement plans or saving for their kid's education.

"So, just to confirm: you're really not interested in investing your life savings with my company. Yes, that's right, the one you just told me you've never heard of? Well, thank you for your time. I'll be sure to send you an email and call you back in a few days anyway!"

After the person I was harassing on the other end of the line had politely told me to 'do one', I'd move on to the next number on my list in the hope that they might be a little more excited by my pension plan banter. On the rare occasion that somebody wanted to discuss my proposal further, a colleague (who actually knew what they were talking about) would go to meet them and discuss these saving plans in more detail.

If this was successful, a deal would be signed and I'd make some money. Or this was the idea. It didn't really work out like this for me though. After a few short months in the job I was no closer to making any money than I was on my first day there. In fact, there were probably kids in Asian sweatshops who'd out-earned me during these three months.

My savings were dwindling each day that I wasn't securing a deal and my social life was pretty much nonexistent too.

Before you get the violins out to play me a sad song though, on reflection I can't say this experience was entirely awful. Maybe the best thing I've done in Brazil came off the back of this telesales job – blagging my way into one of the biggest events in Brazil's fashion calendar, São Paulo Fashion Week.

One afternoon during my lunch hour, I was reading the sort of high-end British online website that featured Paris Hilton wearing a slutty dress. She'd been modeling at the Fashion Week the previous day, and as soon as I saw her picture I had the idea of going to gatecrash the event.

My boss had always told me and my script-reading colleagues that we should go to corporate events, network and try to get contacts. Despite a clothes show clearly not being what he had in mind when he'd suggested this, I somehow managed to persuade him to let my co-worker and I take the afternoon off work to check it out. Not long after he'd agreed, we were attempting to get past one very harassed looking woman outside the entrance to the Fashion Week venue. I should point out that I would never usually try to do this sort of thing, but at this point I was still full of the courage that inspired me to forge a new life in Brazil (plus a desperate need for an afternoon away from my phone). So I explained to this woman that we worked for a prestigious magazine based in London, called *Fashionable UK*.

Granted, this wasn't the most creative magazine name I could have come up with on the spot, but she seemed to buy it. The idea that is – she never admitted to reading my fictitious magazine. I told her that we'd just flown in to Brazil and had been disappointed to find out our passes for the event hadn't been sent to the hotel as our editor had promised. I could see that her face was dripping with suspicion as I explained this, but every question she asked I was seemingly able to answer convincingly enough to satisfy whatever doubts she had. Plus, I have a pair of blue eyes and a genuine English accent, which gives me one up on most other Brazilians trying to blag their way in. So, after questioning us on what exactly we were hoping to get from the show ("a general feel of what's hot and what's not in Brazil," was one of the lines I used, without cringing at myself), she escorted us past the crowds of hipsters and excited fashion students waiting outside the runway show. She then seated us on the front row of the next catwalk event. I couldn't believe it! Just an hour earlier I'd been eating a tuna sandwich at my desk, and there I was on the front row of a world-famous fashion event, about to watch gaunt woman modeling hideous clothes!

After the show I imagined we'd be able to walk around the building and then sneak off, ideally with a few phone numbers of people we could flog pension plans to back in the office. But then we discovered that our passes gave us entry to some big-name fashion magazine parties, all of which had DJs spinning electronic music to people supping free champagne. Naturally we decided to take full advantage of our new journalistic status and indulge in the freebies on offer.

I'd given the woman we'd met on the door the nickname Madge, because she had a huge Madonna headpiece awkwardly resting on her curly mop of hair. As you can see, the telesales job had clearly sapped my creativity for coming up with witty nicknames! Madge had a habit of finding us at these parties and personally making sure we were at each runway show before the lights went down. After the third show of the day she caught up with us to ask if there was any extra material we needed for our article.

Perhaps sensing that we were simply being polite by declining, her eyes fixed on a very dapper-looking fashionista nearby (wearing a *GQ South Africa* badge), and she marched us over to him to ask if he'd mind being interviewed by us. He didn't, and as soon as Madge heard this she went off to speak to someone else, leaving me to conduct an interview. Obviously I'd not interviewed anyone before, so I was genuinely worried that we were about to be rumbled in the face of this seasoned professional. Less than a minute into our 'interview' on Brazil's importance to the world of fashion, I thought he'd sussed us out.

After I'd asked him something about fashion, Mr. GQ stopped what he was saying mid-sentence to stare at me. He contemplated me for a while and as he did this, I became conscious that my cheeks were reddening and that panic was now surely readable in my eyes.

"I'm so sorry. Can I ask you something?"

"That's it! He knows," I thought, and, in that moment, time slowed down, the air became still and I was no longer aware of anything else happening around me.

"Well," he started. "I'm sorry to have to ask this."

I took a deep breath.

"But can we finish this tomorrow? I'm so drunk right now I can barely see straight! Why don't we all head to the *Vogue* lounge and have some drinks there instead?"

Inside the Vogue lounge

A wave of relief instantly hit me. We quickly took him up on his offer and accompanied him into the *Vogue* magazine party, where we were introduced to some of his friends. We did our best not to look impressed by how lavish the party was, like *Vogue* parties were quite normal to us. Really, all I wanted to do was dip my head in the chocolate fountain and take some pictures of the place! It turned out that this guy's friends were international journalists covering the event for various publications, and from what I could gather we'd joined them right in the middle of a discussion about the show we'd all just seen. The woman I was standing next to from a high-end magazine immediately asked me about the show.

"Andrew, I'm really interested in what you thought about the collection on the last runway, especially with you being so familiar with the world of fashion in London. Give me your opinion on it!"

I looked at her thoughtfully, then at my friend and then back at her. I had absolutely no idea what to say. I'd spent most of my time at that last show wondering how these skinny women had enough energy to physically get from one end of the runway to the other without passing out from exhaustion. I'd not paid too much attention to what they'd been wearing. So I blurted out the first thing that came to mind. "I'll be honest with you: I thought those designs were … ugly!"

This woman's face was expressionless at first, but it wasn't long before her head was slowly nodding in appreciation. "I'm so glad someone said that," she said, quietly enough for me to realise the comment was intended to be confidential. "The clothes did nothing to flatter a woman's physique, did they? I just don't think the designer gets women at all!"

Of course I agreed with her, but then deemed it advisable to get the hell away from her before she asked me any more questions (questions that would have exposed me and my friend for the frauds we really were!).

We were found an hour later by Madge at a different magazine party. Seriously, this woman was like one of those puppies who don't take the hint you're just not in the mood to play with them. We were already quite happy where we were with our champagne, but she promptly escorted us to the final runway show of the day: a particularly hideous Halloween inspired collection. There we were seated next to a very enthusiastic looking woman who sniffed a lot and had huge, bulging eyes. She introduced herself to me as a fashion blogger and I told her about my role at *Fashionable UK* magazine. Because I was now a few glasses of champagne into the event, my position there had become a whole lot more exaggerated.

"I have to say I really enjoy reading your articles," she gushed, with enough sincerity for me to forget for a second that I wasn't actually a fashion writer. On reflection, meeting this Scandinavian fan (whose breath absolutely reeked of bullshit) was perhaps the highlight of my very, very short career as a fashion writer.

Picture taken from my front row seat

As strange as this may sound, up until this day at São Paulo Fashion Week I'd become so focused on getting this elusive financial deal signed in the call centre that I'd not really thought too much about what other opportunities were even possible for me in São Paulo. So, in a way, gate crashing the event was a big turning point for me here. It made me consider what else the city had to offer beyond the four magnolia walls of the office, and it helped me to recognise that I'd lost sight of the fact I'd not come to Brazil to cold call people.

It was time for a change.

A few days after watching these skeletons parading down the runway, I handed in my notice and found an English school in need of experienced native instructors. At first it felt like a novelty to be teaching Brazilians who actually wanted to talk to me! A few weeks later I also had a decent amount of money coming in, which meant my relationship with São Paulo changed considerably. I could afford to go out, meet new people and experience more than my previous situation had allowed.

This is not to say that I was blind to the more unusual aspects of life in the city before this though. There are certain elements of Brazilian culture that are unmissable on even the smallest of budgets. A good example of this is the kissing culture. Before I make myself sound incredibly old-fashioned and prudish, I should point out that after four years in Japan I'd grown used to the Japanese way of greeting people. This consisted of bowing a lot and avoiding most forms of physical contact.

Just a fortnight before moving to Brazil I had been saying goodbye to the high school students I'd spent the year teaching. I was asked to give a farewell speech during the final assembly in Japanese, and I was pretty nervous about it. After a lot of practice before the big day my moment in the school hall arrived. Then I gave my well-polished speech to over 400 kids, during what seemed like the longest five minutes of my life. As it finished I was both happy that people seemed to have understood what I was trying to say in Japanese, and relieved to have got it out of the way. I'd not thought too much about the sentimental content of it until a few minutes after the assembly finished, when one of my teenage students came over to see me.

"Andrew," she said, biting on her wobbly bottom lip, "I will miss you." I noticed a solitary tear streaming down her left cheek.

I instinctively threw my arms around her, but when they folded around her tiny frame she didn't hug me back. Instead she simply stood there with her arms locked by her side, crying into my chest. On reflection I'm sure this moment was as awkward for me as it was for her, because neither of us knew how to respond to what the other was doing. I'd completely forgotten that hugging like this was inappropriate in Japan, and my colleague later told me that my student would have not only felt uncomfortable that I was hugging her, but she would have also had the added embarrassment of losing her composure in such a public setting.

With this being one of the lasting memories I took from the end of my time in Japan, I moved to Brazil. In comparison, this place is a parallel universe!

Over here friends think nothing of greeting each other with hugs and kisses, guys offer each other a handshake and a playful slap on the back, and couples kiss each other almost everywhere. I'm really not exaggerating one bit here, I really mean everywhere! On my first ever visit to a Brazilian supermarket I was amazed to see that the couple in front of me in the line for the checkout were so absorbed in their own passion, they looked like they were just moments away from ripping each other's clothes off right there and then, next to the stand of discounted Doritos.

"What is it about shopping for washing powder, milk and cereal that has awoken such passion in them both?" I asked myself. "Can't they wait until they get home?"

If you're coming to Brazil then get ready to see this sort of thing on a regular basis. What still gets me are the couples kissing intensely on the train, even when it is propelled down the tracks and flinging its passengers from side to side. I often see couples full-on snogging in these carriages, as if these people are oblivious to the amount of damage they could do to their teeth. One day I fully expect to see these amorous couples breaking off from their kissing marathons on the trains to spit blood and chipped teeth onto the floor, like something from an apocalypse zombie movie!

Seeing how tactile Brazilians are initially proved to be quite an eye opener. It has certainly taken some time to get used to. At first I felt quite awkward around Brazilians whenever they greeted me with a hug and a kiss, like maybe I needed to see a therapist about my intimacy issues! But I knew this cold response had to change if I was to successfully integrate into Brazilian culture. So, a few weeks into my new teaching role I decided to throw caution to the wind and kiss. With interesting results!

How Not To Kiss In São Paulo

I'd not been teaching at my school that long when I was assigned a morning class starting at 7am. When one of my students came up to greet me each morning, as she entered the room, I knew that when she tilted her head to the side she was expecting me to kiss her cheek. Yet, more often than not, I'd notice that immediately after I'd kissed her, she would pull a bit of a face. I'd then see her trying to subtly rub her cheek where my lips had just landed. I won't lie to you: this *really* confused me. Why go in for a kiss if you don't really want to be kissed in the first place?

Well, after class one day I was talking to the school's receptionist and I asked her for some advice. I wanted to know exactly what I was doing wrong. "Do you think I should stop wetting my lips before I kiss? I mean, do Brazilians usually kiss with slightly wet lips or dry lips?" I thought my question had been sincere enough, but, as soon as I'd asked, the receptionist put her hand over her mouth.

"Do you really kiss people?"

"Well, yes."

"With wet lips?"

"Of course, it's just old people in the UK who kiss with dry lips! Isn't it the same here?"

What started off as a slight chuckle developed into a piercing cackle that was difficult for everyone around us to ignore. After she'd eventually regained her composure, she said that the idea of me slobbering over my student had made her day. In São Paulo kissing is more of a theatrical air kiss and not actually a real kiss. And it is just one kiss. In Rio it is two, and in the north of the country it can be as many as three.

Kissing an immaculately-dressed, middle-aged business woman with wet lips ... well, it was never likely to go down very well. Needless to say, I quickly stopped doing this!

Kissing wasn't the only aspect of life that surprised me here either; my many trips to the supermarket did this too. Generally when I shop for groceries at my local supermarket it takes me a good ten to fifteen minutes to find everything I need, then much longer to pay for it all. This is because the majority of checkout assistants won't be busting their balls to get everyone's shopping scanned and paid for quickly if they can help it!

I was once second in a long queue when the woman on the checkout invited her friends to push in front and get served before me. Then, after a good old catch up with the girls, she eventually started scanning my food. But then she stopped again when her phone started beeping; she'd received a message that she felt compelled to read with my Haribo Gummy Bears still in her hand. There was a huge line behind her, one she can't have been oblivious to; it was one she clearly wasn't all that bothered by. The more supermarkets I've been in the more I've come to appreciate that it isn't just my local that excels in providing awful customer service.

Sometimes if the checkout woman on the till over from you wants to have a chat with the woman serving you, she won't think twice about stopping work for a gossip (whether she has customers or not!). My checkout woman once even put down my bread for a chat, swung round for a natter, then a minute or so later roared with laughter at a joke she'd just been told. The whole time I was standing there willing her to get back to work.

When I asked my students why these women don't seem too bothered about their customers, they simply say, "well, these people don't get paid so much. But if you go to … (they then name an expensive supermarket), they are a little friendlier in there." It is quite interesting how people with low-paid jobs in São Paulo are almost excused for having a relaxed attitude to their work. I couldn't care less how much money these checkout women are earning: I like their full attention and a smile with my loaf of bread, milk and Frosties!

So here's the part about supermarket shopping that I find the most confrontational: paying for it all. If you have the correct change or a card then you are probably going to be OK. However, if you pull a note larger than a 20 out of your pocket, you're likely to be in trouble. What I'm about to describe has happened to me many times, and if you're paying with a large note you too might experience something similar.

The checkout assistant will glare at you in disgust when you pull your large note out, like she's just watched you strangle a puppy. She will then ask if you have change. If you answer that you don't, get ready for further questioning. Checkout assistants are reluctant to accept your first negative answer when it comes to you not having change. I suspect this is because the thing they seem to hate more than their jobs is actually handing over lots of notes and coins.

"Not even (X amount of) *centavos*?"

"No."

"Well, don't you have another form of payment?"

"No."

After saying this, your checkout woman is likely to sigh at you like you have just *really* inconvenienced her life. Actually, problems with change aren't limited to the supermarkets ... a cashier once tried to stare me out when I gave her a 50 real note to pay for my dinner in a shopping centre. She actually stood there and stared at me, like she thought she could intimidate me into giving her a smaller note. Well, I didn't have any other notes, and after telling her I had no change I stared back at 'Miss Salad Creations'! We were like this for a good five seconds until she reluctantly gave in and handed me my change: the change she told me that she didn't have.

Brazilians love their credit and debit cards, which makes sense when you think about it. With crime being so prevalent in the country, having large amounts of cash on you isn't really ideal.

If this 'change' conversation takes place in a large supermarket and the checkout assistant trusts that you really don't have change, a switch will be pressed to light up the till number you're at. Think of this checkout light like the signal used to call Batman, only instead of a rubber-caped superhero coming to your rescue it's going to be a till supervisor on roller skates! Yes, flippin' roller skates!

Despite being here for years now, it still makes me smile when I see one of these supervisors emerging from the depths of the aisles in crash helmets and knee pads, whizzing over to your checkout to provide change.

Roller-skating supervisors don't just come over with money either; you will see them flying over to you when a price check needs to be carried out, or when the assistant on the till makes a mistake with her scanning. For whatever reason checkout assistants aren't usually able to cancel transactions themselves. I suspect this is either because their employers don't trust them, or because supermarkets want your wait in line to be that little bit longer than it really needs to be!

Chapter Three – Teaching Brazilians

Before arriving in São Paulo I'd never really considered working as an English teacher over here. I'd assumed that because there were very few teaching positions advertised for foreign teachers online, there wasn't much of a market for this sort of work here. But with the realisation that my 'career' in finance wasn't working out, I seriously began to look into English teaching as a way to support myself. I was pretty relieved to discover that there are actually a hell of a lot of Brazilians wanting to take classes from native English instructors.

But then São Paulo is the beating financial heart of Brazil, with many multinational companies already established here and many more coming over to set up shop. So this demand for teachers makes sense. Writing emails, conversing with international colleagues, hosting foreign guests and making trips abroad are a way of life for many white-collar workers in the city. In fact, for many of these guys English isn't just a necessity but can potentially be a meal ticket to promotion and further job opportunities. So unsurprisingly there are a lot of Brazilians keen to improve their English skills.

The teaching market isn't just limited to these guys either; I've had students ranging from housewives to fashion models (Repeat after me; 'turn to the left and give me sexy!'), university students to journalists, and TV actresses to priests. It would be fair to say that the majority of the classes I teach are given to business types though, generally in company offices before the working day has started, straight after work or during lunch breaks.

With security in this city being the way it is, I'm required to identify myself at a company's reception desk with some ID each time I enter a building. As I pass my identification over I let the receptionist know that the "*professor de inglês*" has arrived. That's right; if you're coming over here to teach, you can skip the PhD course. Thanks to a false cognate you're going to be known as a professor instead of just an instructor!

Top 5 Mistakes Brazilians Make In English

After doing this job for about four years now I've obviously corrected a number of mistakes in class, some more amusing than others. I'm not about to share my favourites because I want to poke fun of the people who made them; I've made enough mistakes with Portuguese myself to understand that this is just part and parcel of studying another language (Don't even get me started on the time I ordered 'grilled dick' instead of 'grilled bread' at the local bakery in front of my friends!). If you're a Brazilian who is studying English, or if you're a foreigner about to come over to Brazil with the intention of speaking to Brazilians, this section of the book might help you avoid a few potentially embarrassing situations.

5.   **The Adulterers**

"I've been single for a while," said one of my students in response to being asked if he was married. He then added in a slightly despondent tone, "I had two affairs last year, but they didn't work out."

My initial thought was just, "*Wow!*" I mean, I wasn't about to judge this ~~home wrecker~~ guy for brazenly telling me he likes relationships with married women, but there were three of his colleagues also listening in. Obviously I thought they would be looking slightly uneasy at this revelation, but, much to my surprise, as I glanced around I noticed that they were all looking at him sympathetically.

I'd not been in Brazil for all that long, and at this point I thought to myself: "Hang on a minute, do Brazilians think nothing to having extramarital relationships? This can't be right, can it?"

By now, I was curious, "sooooooo, is it, erm, common for Brazilians to have relationships with married people?" A few seconds later the silence was broken by one of these students. "Sorry, but why are you asking us this?"

After a slightly awkward conversation it turns out the word 'affair' over here means something different to the English meaning. To me, the word 'affair' means someone who is having some kind of extramarital relationship, but in Brazil it means you are having a relationship.

4. You vs. He/She

Quite a lot of the beginner and intermediate students I've taught in Brazil have found pronouns to be a bit of a problem, which can lead to some interesting misunderstandings. Let me give you an example of one of these. I once gave a class that focused on personal appearance and my student was asked to describe a famous person:

"So what does Angelina Jolie look like?"
"She is very beautiful. She is very tall."
"OK."
"She has long, brown hair."
"Yep."
"And you have very beautiful lips!"
"Well, thank you … but let's get back to describing Angelina!"

It took my student a good few seconds to notice his mistake, and as soon as he realised he began to backtrack. "No, not you, I meant Angelina! Angelina has beautiful lips, not you!"

"Too late, you've said it now," I joked. Mid-pout.

3.   Are You A Bitch Lover!?!

Although the alphabet in English is written as it is in Portuguese, when spoken many of these letters sound different. To a Portuguese speaker the letter 'e' is pronounced like the English letter 'i'.

One day in class (quite out of the blue), a beginner student asked me this: "Do you like bitches?" Another of the students in class rushed to point out her mistake, perhaps imagining I was about to give her an honest answer. Of course, she hadn't meant to ask me about my love of hoes; she'd meant 'beaches'.

This mistake seems to be one that the majority of English-speaking Brazilians are familiar with, so if a Brazilian uses the word 'beach' mid-conversation, don't be surprised if they look really intensely at you immediately after saying it. It's likely that they are looking at you like this to check their pronunciation has been correct. Another word that proves quite challenging to get right (often with comic results) is the word 'sheet'. I once had a student tell me that he was looking at the shit I gave him in the previous class and had a question about it!

I'd be lying if I told you the difficulties Brazilians have with the 'e' sound made my list for this reason alone. Oh no! Sometimes it is coupled with another pronunciation mistake. Portuguese speakers also have difficulties pronouncing the 'th' sound in English; they don't use this sound in their own language so they often pronounce the 'th' simply as a 't'.

One morning I was waiting for my students to arrive for our 7am class. The first of my students to arrive was an elderly woman who always looked very glamorous (not at all like the other students, who often looked like the living dead as they stumbled through the door, anything up to 30 minutes late).

"I'm always impressed that you arrive on time for class," I said to her. "You must wake up very early. Tell me about your morning routine."

"Well, I wake up at around 5.30am, take a shower … and then brush my tits before I have breakfast."

"Sorry … you brush what?"

"My tits!"

I fought so hard to repress a laugh as she repeated herself, but I couldn't help it. I was picturing this professional-looking woman combing knots out of her hairy tits after a shower! Obviously she didn't mean tits (or at least, I didn't think she did!); she'd meant teeth. She brushes her teeth on a morning. I'm not quite sure if she ever brushes her tits, but it didn't stop me thinking about her doing this for the rest of our class!

2. "Do You Want To See My Fantasy?"

I once gave a class just after Carnival to two students − a man and a woman both in their late thirties. The class started with me asking the guy what he'd done during Carnival:

"I performed in a samba school parade. It was such a fantastic experience!"

"That sounds great," I remarked. "Tell me more about it."

He looked at me with this huge grin spreading across his face, and then he turned to look at the woman sat beside him. He hesitated for a few seconds before continuing. Unbeknown to me, he was just seconds away from giving me one of my most uncomfortable classroom experiences, *ever*!

"OK, do you want to see my fantasy?"

"Excuse me!?!" I asked, with the smile on my face dropping ever so slightly.

"Do you want to see my fantasy?" he repeated. I had a feeling that's exactly what he'd just asked me. Then without prompting he said, "One moment, I'll find a picture of it for you".

I sat in stunned silence with about a million thoughts flying through my mind. "He can't be? He's not really about to show me something obscene in class, is he!?!" As he flicked through the images in his phone I looked over at the woman sat next to him. She seemed fairly nonchalant that he may have been about to show us something he found arousing. Like this type of thing was normal, like he always shows his 'fantasy pictures' to everyone back in the office!

"I've found it."

I'm not gonna lie to you, right there and then I feared the worst.

"How funny!", my other student giggled.

Funny!?! Well now I was *really* interested. Just what was it!?! He turned his phone around to reveal a small image of himself during the carnival dressed in traditional carnival attire. I was as confused as I was relieved.

So, in this class I learnt that in Brazilian Portuguese, the word 'fantasy' usually refers to a costume, not necessarily to someone's sexual desires.

1.   **My Student's Favourite Slags**

It had been a long day, and by the time I'd got to my final group of students I was pretty tired. In this group was a young woman who kicked our class off by telling everyone about a film she'd seen the night before: "It was great, and I watched it without the Portuguese subtitles. It was quite difficult to understand everything in English, but I recognised a few of the slags."

"I'm sorry," I said. "What did you recognise?"

"A few of the slags. Why are you smiling?"

Again, I had a feeling that was exactly what she'd said.

"Well, who were these slags you recognised?" I asked, desperately trying to suppress a loud belly laugh, but also trying to retain a sense of professionalism.

"Who? Sorry, I don't understand!"

"Well, what do you mean by 'slags'?"

"Slags are informal English, aren't they?"

"Erm, no!" Unfortunately, by now I was really laughing as I pointed out that the word she was looking for was not slag, but slang.

"Well, what is a slag?" she asked.

"Be careful with your pronunciation here, because 'slag' has a completely different meaning to 'slang'," I said, totally trying to avoid the question.

"Yes, now I know. But what is a slag?" The conversation suddenly stopped being funny for me because now I had to explain. "Well, a slag is British English for a woman who enjoys sex with many different men. It's a derogatory term."

"Oh!" she responded without so much as a smile. "And does the woman get paid for having sex with men?"

"Well, no, a slag isn't a prostitute," I replied.

My student then cleared her throat, leaned into the table and looked straight into my eyes.

"Tell me, what is derogatory about a woman who enjoys sex with men if that woman doesn't charge for it?"

With four students now staring at me, waiting for my response, I struggled to think of a good answer. Feeling the pressure, I was aware that my face had begun to turn a deep shade of pink (the same colour pink I once saw my mum turning when she'd got to the supermarket checkout and realised she'd left her purse at home).

"I think by your definition, that makes me a slag!"

If ever there was a time that it would have been hugely inappropriate to agree with a student, here it was. "Do you know what? I think we've had enough talk about slags for one day. So let's open our textbooks to page…."

My Most Awkward Classroom Experience

Whilst these mistakes have certainly given me some memorable classroom moments, none have quite topped the incident I'm about to describe. Everything I'm about to describe to you now is true, except the parts I've made up (namely, anything that would allow someone to identify this student. He could crush me with one hand!).

I'd been asked by my school to substitute for a teacher for a few weeks as he'd gone on holiday. At the time my schedule for Tuesday mornings was pretty empty, and, despite being warned that this student was likely to be 'different' from the others, I gladly accepted the extra classes. The guy I'd been sent to teach was into Muay Thai in a big way, had arms that would've made Popeye envious and had an incredibly deep, authoritative voice. Unsurprisingly, he intimidated the hell out of me!

Unfortunately for me, he seemed to be well aware of this. "You took the subway here?" he once asked before waiting for me to answer in the affirmative. "I sometimes ride it with my children on a weekend, just to let them see how the poor people in this city live."

"Ohhhhhhh, right," I replied after a few seconds of silence. This invited a teasing smirk to play across his lips and then he greedily enjoyed watching me squirm in front of him. This sort of exchange occurred during each and every class, so much so that on the day of our last class, I'd psyched myself up and told myself I wasn't going to get tongue-tied in front of him. I walked into his office feeling prepared for whatever he was going to throw at me.

Only as it turns out, I really wasn't. But not for any of the reasons I'd imagined.

In the middle of our class I asked him a question, one that prompted him to swing his oversized leather chair away from me and towards his office window to consider his answer. After thinking about it for a good ten seconds he slowly turned the chair round to face me again. I couldn't help but think he was just a cat and fake Russian accent away from looking like a great Bond villain.

 "So, I know where my favourite restaurant is …"

Before he'd had the chance to continue though, his phone rang. He briefly held out the palm of his hand in my direction as he picked it up. I'm not sure what my student was trying to prevent me from doing, but like an obedient pet I sat and waited for him to finish his call. After a few minutes I had his attention. "So, where were we?" he asked, sounding like he'd only just remembered how utterly bored he was.

"Your favourite restaurant."
"Ah yes, it's near here. It's quite cheap, there are many alternative people who go there and even jealous people."

"Jealous people?" I repeated, whilst theatrically raising my eyebrows slowly in the hope that this might make him rethink what he'd just said.

"Yes, jealous people," he asserted, with a strange pronunciation of the word 'jealous'. "I often go to restaurants where there are jealous people."

To let him know how strange I found this, I feigned the sort of enthusiastic surprise usually given by actors in a pantomime, "*Reeeeally*?" By doing so I imagined he'd rethink what he'd just said and correct himself.

"Do you have a problem with jealous people?"

"I guess so," I replied. "I don't really feel comfortable around them. I prefer to go to more relaxing places, places without a negative atmosphere."

For the first time since I'd known this student he looked flustered, stunned even. It was as if he couldn't quite believe what he was hearing. I'd never seen him with his cool composure quite so ruffled before. I remember thinking, at that moment, that if he was a Bond villain he'd definitely have pressed a button under his desk to swing my chair back into a pool of ravenous sharks.

"Well, I have no problem with jealous people," he continued, only this time his voice was a little louder. "No problem with them *at all*. In fact, some of my closest friends are gay."

I genuinely had no idea why he was so bothered about me not liking jealous people, or even what his gay friends had to do with this snotty little restaurant he was telling me about. Despite teaching English at this point for over a year and a half and becoming well versed in common mistakes made by Brazilians speaking English, I couldn't for the life of me figure out where this misunderstanding was coming from.

After a few seconds of us looking uncomfortably at each other, I asked him what he understood by the word 'jealous'.

"I understand 'jealous' to mean gay, lesbian and their sympathisers." And in that moment it all made perfect sense.

The letter 'J' in Portuguese sounds like the English letter 'G', and acronyms here are sometimes said like words instead of individual letters. VIP is a prime example of this, and is pronounced 'veepee'. I'd never heard GLS (the Brazilian equivalent of LGBT) being pronounced like 'jealous' before (or even since come to think of it), so this was quite new for me.

"Now I understand," I said, almost relieved to have understood what he'd been trying to say. Yet his serious expression remained as I told him where this misunderstanding had come from. He made it quite clear that this feeling of relief was not one shared by both of us though. He was someone who would suspiciously question all of the new words I'd taught him by consulting Google Translate ("Ah yes, so you are correct with that one"), so I knew that he wasn't going to be entirely convinced by the explanation I'd offered. Then it dawned on me that he must have interpreted what I was saying as a confession that I had a problem with gay people.

I could have tried to explain that I really don't have an issue with anyone identifying themselves as belonging to the GLS/Jealous/LGBT community, but I knew that he would have again enjoyed watching me look uncomfortable doing so. So, I swiftly instructed him to take out his textbook and to turn to the page we were going to be looking at during the class. I raised my eyes when I'd opened my book to look at him, and found that, instead of him opening his book, he'd been sitting there glaring at me with dead eyes the whole time!

The class never really recovered from this moment, and to say that the next hour and fifteen minutes proved to be uncomfortable would be a bit of an understatement. On reflection this was a bit of a shame, given that I'd only wanted to know where his favourite restaurant was. Instead I'd inadvertently made myself sound like a massive homophobe!

Being Outsmarted by a Seven-Year-Old

I used to teach a seven year old with an exceptionally high level of English, and in one of our classes we were playing a board game. Right in the middle of this game I looked up at him and noticed that he was no longer focusing on his next move. Instead he was looking directly at me.

"Andrew," he said, "why do you have a *really* small head and a really *big* nose?"

"I don't have a small head," I said, defiantly. On reflection, this must have sounded more like I was trying to convince myself than him.

"Oh Andrew, of course you have a small head!" was his response, and he said this like I was a fool for even suggesting otherwise. At that, I noticed a cheeky glint in his eye. He'd obviously just realised a new way to mock me in future classes. After this conversation he gleefully brought up the size of my head at least a few times every time I taught him.

We used to play Jenga in our classes too, alongside some pre-written questions that he needed to ask every time he pulled out a piece. On some of these pieces were question marks, and the rule was that when he pulled out one of these, he could ask me anything he wanted. So a few weeks after this conversation about my head had taken place, this happened:

"I have a question," he said, seconds after removing a piece. I knew what was coming, but I had to respect the pre-agreed rules of the Jenga game.

"OK, what is it!?!" I asked hesitantly.

"Why is … your head … soooooooo small?"

At that he fell about laughing, appreciating his own joke to the point of almost hyperventilating. I sat and waited for him to regain his composure (now with a very stern look on my face) before continuing.

When he eventually stopped I told him not to talk about the size of my head any more. "It's not funny," I said, trying to sound genuinely hurt. Then I didn't hear anything more about it for the rest of the class.

The next week, though, he was back to talking about the size of my head. "But it's *sooooooo* small," he teased. Feeling frustrated, I said in quite a matter-of-fact way, "Look! If you don't stop I'm going to tell your mother." Of course, I wasn't going to say anything to his mum. I mean he was only seven years old; I'd have looked ridiculous!

"Tell her what?" he asked with a deliberate theatrical pause. I could see that his eyes were already laughing at what he was about to say next. Like an award-winning comedian he was just waiting for the right moment to deliver his punch line.

"Are you going to tell my mum … that you have a *really* small head!?!"

Again, he laughed hysterically whilst I sat there getting my (not so large) head around the fact that I'd just been owned by a seven year old!

Chapter Four – Going Out In São Paulo

After teaching for a few weeks I finally started to see some money coming in, which meant I could begin to enjoy São Paulo in the way I'd previously hoped to. One of the first things I wanted to do with my wages was to follow the advice of my students and sample some of the city's vibrant nightlife. São Paulo may be a city famous for its business, but come the weekend there are a whole lot of hardworking residents looking to relax and let off some serious steam.

Beer

First, I'll explain my experience of going out for a beer over here. When you order a beer in a simple bar in Brazil (or a *boteco* as they're known in Portuguese), unless you've specifically asked for a can, you're likely to be given a large bottle in a cooler. You will then be asked how many glasses you'd like to go with it. You see, when you're with friends this bottle of beer is to be shared out amongst you all. It would be social suicide to sit there and drink this all by yourself! Being British and incredibly manly (honestly!) I have to confess that I prefer my beer to be served in a pint glass. This is something you don't really get over here, unless you're in an Irish themed pub. Instead, the bartender will bring over some tumbler-sized glasses for you and your party to share your beer out into. These are a bit of a necessity when it's warm here because the beer in these small glasses shouldn't take you long to drink. For this reason you're unlikely to find yourself drinking a glass of lukewarm beer. I can confidently say that (politics aside) with the exception of being beaten by Argentina in an important football game, Brazilians hate nothing more than drinking warm beer.

During my first year in São Paulo, myself and twelve of my Brazilian friends descended onto the coastal city of Ubatuba for a long weekend. Being the only foreigner in the group I often found myself being offered half drunken cans of lager. "It's too hot for me," my friends would complain, "but I know foreign people like hot beer so you can have the rest of my can." The first few times this happened I naturally questioned if I was being tricked into drinking something truly awful. Then I'd drink it, tell them I thought the beer was still cold, then see them staring suspiciously at me.

Since moving to Brazil I've had many people ask me if it's true that British people enjoy hot beer, and then I've had to explain that we prefer our lager to be cold but not ice cold. From the conversations I've had I think some Brazilians have this misguided idea that people from the UK like their beer hot. As if we ask our bartender to stick it in the microwave so it can be heated up a little before serving.

When going out for a drink here, it is also worth noting that many bars and restaurants will serve up their version of a draught beer known as a *chopp*. For anyone thinking of coming out to Brazil and drinking one of these I'll tell you something in advance. Whilst it might taste great, it also comes with a big head. As a Brit I always feel like I'm being ripped off whenever I get an unnecessary layer of foam on top of my beer. That's usually at least one mouthful of beer you've paid for that you're missing out on (who, me? Tight?). However, there is no denying that on a hot day, once you've got past this layer of foam, the *chopp* definitely hits that thirst quenching spot!

Randomly in São Paulo, you aren't limited just to bars, restaurants and clubs when you fancy going out for a beer either. Oh no! São Paulo has one more popular venue that younger people in particular like to flock to.

The petrol station.

And no, I'm not kidding!

On any given weekend in São Paulo, it's pretty much a given that there will be a crowd gathered on petrol station forecourts just yards away from the petrol pumps. Here, tables and chairs are set out for people to use, allowing them to sit amongst the cars and petrol fumes with a beer in one hand and maybe even a cigarette in the other (that's right, people are partial to a cigarette on the petrol garage forecourt too). Surprisingly over here, smoking at the petrol station isn't seen as being amazingly dangerous or even an activity only enjoyed by adrenaline junkies. The beer isn't that cheap at the garages so I'm not really sure what the appeal is. But if you're in town and fancy a beer and a lungful of car fumes, the petrol garage should satisfy this craving!

Clubbing

If you've had enough to drink, the next place on your agenda may well be a nightclub. Nestled away in Latin America's largest city are some amazing clubs; São Paulo has so much to offer in the way of clubbing that you're really quite spoilt for choice when it comes to choosing a place to party your night away. I found out on my first night out here, though, the experience is a little different to the one I used to enjoy back in England.

As I waited in line to get into a club (on my first proper night out on the town) I distinctly remember looking blankly at the beefcake guarding the entrance to the nightclub doors. I really wanted to understand what he was saying to me, but it was glaringly obvious to both of us that my vocabulary bank of about ten words was of no use whatsoever. My face screwed up as he continued talking, but luckily my Brazilian friend behind me was able to offer a translation.

"He wants to see your ID."

"My ID!" I thought to myself, "He wants to see my ID!?! Really? This is absolutely *amazing*!"

Although I'd been told to bring my ID out with me, this was the first time in over ten years that I'd been asked to show it on my way into a nightclub. In the clubs in the UK, you only really get asked for it if you look under 21. So, being close to the wrong side of 30 and with an ever receding hairline, I thought my days of needing to prove my age were well and truly behind me. I felt quite flattered to have been asked. "That's right Andrew!" I told myself as I got out my passport, "you've *still* got it!"

After I'd been waved into the club I turned around to look at my friend with a huge grin. But I saw that he was also being asked to show his passport. The woman stood in line behind him was pulling out her ID ready for inspection too (even though her face looked a little bit like a well-worn leather handbag). My ego deflated pretty swiftly when I worked out that I hadn't been asked for my identification because of my Peter Pan looks, but just because everybody needs to show it!

Once inside the club I waited in another line to speak to someone sat behind a glass window. Here I was asked the following question: "*Consumação ou entrada*?" What the member of staff was asking me here was if I wanted to pay a cover charge or take the more expensive *consumação* option (a literal translation of this word is 'consumption').

Let me give you an example of how this works. Let's imagine that the nightclub you've just entered charges a R$20 cover to get in, but it's R$40 if you go for the consumption option. If you pay *entrada*, you'll need to pay R$20 plus whatever you consume in drinks. But if you opt for consumption you can use the R$40 to drink, and if you consume this amount or more then you don't need to pay a cover charge. If you purchase less than R$40 worth of drinks though, you will still pay R$40. So it's actually worthwhile taking the *consumação* option if you plan on drinking a decent amount.

In exchange for your ID number and your answer to the "*consumação ou entrada*?" question, unless you're at an 'open bar' party (which means all you can drink), you're going to be given a card on which you can get your drinks at the bar. This card works as a way to record your bar tab and is either going to come in a paper or plastic form. Personally I prefer the paper cards because, after ordering your drink at the bar, the bartender will physically score off how much you've spent on this card with a pen. This means you can check yourself how much your tab will come to at any point during the evening. However, the plastic cards don't give you this luxury. So, after you've had your plastic card scanned or swiped through the computer system to record your drinks, unless you are able to ask them how much you've spent in Portuguese, you'll need to keep a mental note of how much your bill is going to come to. And let's be honest, after a few hours of dancing and drinking, remembering how much of a tab you've run up is easier said than done!

So, what happens if you find you've lost your card or don't have enough money to settle your bill? Well, this is a good question and one I'm fortunately not in a position to be able to answer. Having heard a few horror stories though, what I will say is this: be careful and guard that card with your life!

On the plus side, with this card system you're going to find yourself being served quicker than you would back home because the bartender isn't also dealing with change. Personally, the last thing I want to be doing after standing in a long queue to get into a club is to stand in another very long queue to wait for my drink. So, in my humble opinion I think that this system is a good idea. But do you know what? Even though I've been living in São Paulo for some time, lines still get to me. Unfortunately, waiting in queues is likely to be a big part of most people's time when they're in Brazil.

Queues

I'd say Brazilians seem to have an unbelievably high tolerance for queues, more so than back home. Before moving here I assumed that Brits were amazing at standing in them; it is something we pride ourselves on, after all. "Brits know how to queue," I've heard quite often. But we have nothing on Brazilians!

I'm pretty sure that most of the time a Brazilian will join a line just for the fun of it, without knowing what is waiting for them at the front. It isn't just their ability to stand in line for so long that impresses me, but also the way people usually don't hurl abuse at others who push in.

"Oh no, we wouldn't say anything," have said many of my friends when I've asked them why they let people queue jump. "It's just not worth it. It's just not our way of doing things."

Brazilians might look incredibly passionate and feisty whenever the cameras are on them during international football matches, but stick these same people in a long queue with a few people pushing in, and they're likely to say nothing. Queues and pushers-in are like Kryptonite for Brazilians; for whatever reason they usually just grin and bear them. So expect a line or two with people pushing in when you're on a night out!

Spirits

Once inside the club, when you get to the bar it is worth noting that if you decide on a spirit, the 35ml measures adhered to quite stringently in the UK really aren't taken seriously here. For things like shots, a measure seems to be however big the shot glasses are (these glasses can vary in size) and because some of these glasses are quite big, the alcohol itself can be a bit of a challenge to swallow in one mouthful. On more than one occasion I've needed two gulps to get my shot down, which really surprised me, given that I have quite a sizable mouth!

If shots aren't your thing and instead you ask for a spirit with a mixer, your bartender will probably make use of the jigger to measure out your alcohol (this isn't just a word I was surprised even existed before looking it up, but it is also a word used to describe those metal sprit measures you've probably seen in most bars or clubs). Your bartender may then add a splash more spirit in your glass; some will follow this first splash up with a few more splashes, and then there are those who will add a whole lot more than that … depending on how cute they find you/ how engrossed they are in their conversations with other bartenders. Some won't even bother with the jigger and just measure out the drink going on their own (often generous) instincts. This means your drink could end up being a whole lot stronger than you'd anticipated. I'll leave it to you to decide if having a strong drink is a good thing or not, but, what I will say is this: when it comes to drinking shots and spirits in São Paulo, you have been warned!

Because very few self-respecting clubs in the city get going before midnight, many won't finish until around 5 or 6 in the morning. You're likely to find that a lot of people party until at least the time the metro opens (which in São Paulo is just before 5am), so I've found that a night out on the town here requires stamina!

When you've danced until your feet hurt, maybe drank a little bit too much than you should've, and a sudden urge to sleep, eat or both has just hit you … what's next? Well, now it's time to pay the balance on your card and get the hell out of there. Unfortunately, when you want to leave the club, the chances are so too will everyone else. This is the part of the evening where you need to patiently stand in a line (again) and wait. Sometimes the queue might be no more than a few minutes long … other times, well, let's not even go there!

"Andrew, why are you annoyed about waiting in this line?" a Brazilian friend once asked me as we stood in a never-ending line that was meandering very slowly towards the exit. "This is a really good opportunity!"

"Good opportunity?" I asked, "A good opportunity for what?"

"The line is absolutely a good time to flirt!"

I have yet to meet my soul mate whilst standing in a line at 5am, but to this day I still smile when I remember my friend's optimism as I'm waiting.

When your bill is settled you're going to receive a stamp on your card or given a second card to give to the bouncers. These are effectively your tickets out of there. So, whatever you do don't lose them! After handing whatever you've been given over to the 'Men In Black' on the door, you'll be free to leave, having just (hopefully) survived a night out in São Paulo.

So, that's going out for a beer and going out to party covered, but there's one further aspect of the nightlife here that is hugely important for Brazilians: the music. This brings me neatly onto the next chapter.

Chapter Five – Music

"We've told you who our favourite English singers and bands are," said one of my students in the middle of our early evening class. "Now it's your turn! Which Brazilian artists do you like?"

"Eeeerrrrrrm …" I responded thoughtfully, before looking up at the polystyrene panels in the classroom ceiling and hoping that they would inspire an answer. "What Brazilian singer … or band … do … I … like?" I asked this to myself out loud, with my tone suggesting I would need some time to narrow my decision down. The truth was, I was going to struggle to think of a single one.

So I started to think of all the Latin artists I knew. "Shakira, she's Colombian. Gloria Estefan, American? Wait, I'm not sure where she is from but it doesn't matter, she's definitely not Brazilian. Surely I know some more, Ricky Martin?" Well, regardless of where he is from, I wasn't about to tell this class of business executives that I was a fan of the guy famous for singing 'She Bangs'! With four pairs of eyes looking expectantly at me and the seconds ticking away, I started to feel the pressure. This is when I nervously began to laugh.

"What are you laughing at?" one student asked. There were no two ways about this; I needed to come clean.

I'd already been living in Brazil for five months at this point, and I really should have known a lot more about Brazilian music than I did. Yet, when I'd finally started making enough money to go out, instead of going to the clubs and bars that were playing Brazilian music, I partied in the many electronic clubs São Paulo has to offer. So, it wasn't that I'd consciously avoided Brazilian music; I'd just not made much of an effort to go out and discover what it was all about.

"Well, you see, I don't really like samba," I began, "it all sounds the same to me. And there aren't really many other types of Brazilian music, are there? Your singers and bands aren't famous in England, so to answer your question I don't really think I like any Brazilian artists."

The wall of silence that followed this comment was as deafening as it was awkward. My students just sat and glared at me until eventually one leant across the table, grabbed my notepad and said: "OK teacher, now it's time for *your* homework. You need to look up these Brazilian artists on YouTube and let us know which ones you like in our next class." She turned to the other students and together they compiled a list of singers and bands for me to check out.

That evening as I listened to each one on the list, I can honestly say that it was only then that I began to appreciate the world of Brazilian music. There are a lot of types of Brazilian music I was unfamiliar with before this day, from MPB to Axe, Pagode to Forro. Instead of describing each of these genres, what I'll do in this chapter is give you my take on the Brazilian styles I consider to be good, bad and just downright ugly! So let's kick things off with:

The Good – Samba

A few samba artists were on my students list because (and forgive me for pointing out the bloody obvious here) samba is extremely popular in Brazil. If I'm being completely honest though, it took me a good two years to 'get' its appeal. I mean, I liked it but I wasn't able to differentiate one song from another. Not wanting to offend any Brazilians with this admission I kept this thought to myself, until one evening when I was a few drinks into a staff party. Here I broached the subject with one of my American colleagues.

"Seriously, you're not alone in thinking samba songs all sound the same," she assured me. "I've been in Brazil now for over 20 years and they *still* all sound almost identical to me." Hearing this was somewhat comforting because, whilst I was open to the idea of enjoying samba, I'd resigned myself to thinking I was just someone who didn't understand it. A few Brazilians have pointed out that they feel this way about British guitar music too, that to them it all sounds very repetitive. So I thought that enjoying samba was maybe a cultural thing.

This all changed the day my housemate invited me to join her at a free samba party near our house. I accepted her invitation but wasn't really expecting a whole lot from it. When we walked towards a square full of people dancing and drinking around a live samba band though, my attitude towards it changed instantly. There was a great energy at this party and the crowd gathered there seemed very unpretentious. What struck me most was that these people were of different generations and walks of life, simply there to enjoy the music and have a great time.

I didn't see anybody judging anybody else for dancing badly either, which was a bonus for me because it made me (and my 'Mr. Bean at a rave' style of samba dancing) feel a whole lot more comfortable. You see, I really can't samba. I've attempted it several times, but then, after about ten minutes of some patient Brazilian teaching me the steps, I give up. I figure I badly look like someone who just needs to use the bathroom! Nevertheless, going to these parties has definitely enhanced my enjoyment of the style and I certainly feel like I appreciate it a whole lot more now.

The Good – Bossa Nova

When I asked my Portuguese teacher about the Brazilian music he enjoyed, he answered without so much as pausing for thought, "Bossa nova."

"You've heard the bossa nova song 'The Girl from Ipanema', right?" he enquired.

"Girl from Ipanema? Isn't that samba?" I thought to myself. Well, I later found out that it isn't. Whilst bossa nova has its roots in samba, if you were to compare the two genres, bossa nova has more of a classic, laid-back and jazzy vibe to it.

"Everything about 'The Girl from Ipanema' is just fantastic," he continued, "the lyrics, the melody, the rhythm. It all comes from a golden era of Brazilian music. You had the likes of Chico Boarque, Elis Regina, Tom Jobim and Gilberto Gil. They don't really make quality music like this anymore," he sighed.

Coincidentally, a few weeks after this conversation one of my friends invited me to a free concert held to celebrate the music of the late Brazilian singer, Tom Jobim. This guy was one of the composers of 'Garota de Ipanema', the song believed to be the second most recorded song of all time behind The Beatles 'Yesterday'. Jobim is regarded by many here as incredibly influential to the world of Brazilian music. So, this tribute concert, held on a sleepy Sunday afternoon, was absolutely packed.

A selection of his most popular hits was interpreted by Grammy award-winning singer Vanessa da Mata, who took a quick break about an hour into the gig. As soon as she'd left the stage, old video footage of Jobim singing 'Garota de Ipanema' was played to the thousands in attendance. Tom Jobim wasn't singing this song alone though; he was crooning with Ol' Blue Eyes himself, Frank Sinatra. Prior to moving to Brazil the version sung by Sinatra was the one I was most familiar with. However, the longer I'd been here the more exposure to Jobim's Portuguese version I'd had. So, when I realised that each of the singers would be singing the song in their native language, I was quite curious to hear the collaboration.

"Listen to Frank Sinatra," said one of my friends a minute into the video. As I turned to look at him I noticed a look of absolute disdain etched on his face. He was not impressed. "Frank Sinatra sounds *really* shit!" He said this with such a strong emphasis on the word 'really' that his opinion sounded so final.

I then looked around at the rest of my friends and was shocked to see that they were nodding in agreement, effectively confirming that they also thought Frank sounded 'really shit'. Had I not said anything I'm pretty sure that everyone would have returned to their zombie-like states to watch the rest of the video. But I wasn't about to let this one lie.

"Sorry?" I remarked a little melodramatically (a little bit like when Keanu Reeves tried to sound sincere in *The Matrix*). "Did you just say that you thought Frank Sinatra sounds … shit?"

Of course, I knew the answer to this. I just wanted to hear verbal confirmation. "Absolutely," said my friend with an air of superiority on the matter. "Frank Sinatra is just growling (he didn't actually say the word 'growling', but from the Exorcist-like noises he was making I'm pretty sure this is what he was getting at), he doesn't sound nearly as good as Jobim."

"Andrew, this is Tom Jobim," he said whilst pointing over to the big screen and almost hitting the woman's head in front of us. "As one of the greatest singers in the world. Sinatra shouldn't have even tried to sing 'The Girl From Ipanema' with him." Now I'm no big Frank Sinatra fan, but I've always respected him as being one of the all time greats. So to hear him being trashed as if he were Justin Bieber or Will.i.am really surprised me. As the video finished everyone applauded and Vanessa de Mata reappeared on stage to continue the concert (now strangely draped in what looked like a white duvet cover with holes cut out to accommodate her head and arms). No more was said about Frank and Tom until after the concert on the train ride home, where I raised the subject again.

"I'm not saying I don't like Frank Sinatra," reasoned my friend, "because I do. It's just that his voice isn't melodic enough to sing 'The Girl From Ipanema'." The next day in class I asked my students for their opinions on the versions sung by both artists. Naturally, they unanimously told me that they preferred Jobim's version (although many also cited other versions of the song they enjoyed, with Astrud Gilberto's version proving very popular).

"Andrew, the way Jobim sings it is just beautiful," said my first student of the day. He then enthusiastically burst into song, before adding, "You see, it's just more beautiful in Portuguese. It loses something when it's sung in English. Besides, it's a Brazilian song not an American one." A number of the students I asked that day also channeled their inner-Glee to sing the first two lines to me, like they were actually Tom Jobim. By doing this they didn't just showcase some questionable vocal abilities, but also a clear passion for Jobim's Portuguese version.

Over here in the land where he is regarded so affectionately it makes sense that his version is appreciated to the extent it is. This then got me wondering: is the song more beautiful to Brazilians when it is sung in Portuguese? Do they consider it more superior because it is the most famous song to have come out of Brazil, and therefore culturally important enough not to be sung by anyone other than a Brazilian? And on the subject of Sinatra sounding 'shit', I know that music is subjective but I hadn't ever expected the music of Ol' Blue Eyes to be!

When I wrote a blog post on this subject I was grateful to receive a particularly insightful comment from one of my readers. "Sinatra is not called 'The Voice' without reason," said Jose Ribeiro. "He's one of the greatest crooners humanity has produced. He has an extraordinary voice, but his real great plus is his personality which he projects when he sings. *That* makes his performances so special. Jobim has a sweet, gentle way of singing and a beautiful voice too. But, in this case, the poet makes the biggest difference."

"In Sinatra's song and performance, we visualize a blue guy who was rejected/not noticed by a beautiful woman. He's sad and one can almost perceive some self-pity from a lost love while he sips a scotch in a NYC nightclub. The Brazilian lyrics create the image of someone sitting at a sidewalk table, sipping beer and having a good time with friends when that stunning gal walks by, swinging those marvellous hips on the way to the sea. And she is oblivious to the admiration and desire she creates when she passes by. No sadness, no lost love, just admiration and a natural unfulfilled desire."

The importance of each of the performer's personalities wasn't something I'd really thought too much about when interpreting their versions of the song. So attending this concert certainly gave me food for thought on what the bossa nova style was all about.

The Bad – Sertanejo

Right (I'm now taking a deep breath, cracking my knuckles and stretching), let's do this!

I've tried to enjoy sertanejo, I really have. It's the most played genre of music on Brazilian radio, so I've had plenty of opportunities to embrace it. But for whatever reason I just haven't been able to. Perhaps it's because country music isn't popular in the UK, or maybe it has something to do with the hideous accordions that feature so heavily in a lot of these songs. In my day-to-day life in São Paulo I hear a lot of accordion riffs being pumped out of bars near my house and on car stereos, and I just can't seem to appreciate them in the same way many Brazilians do. But maybe I wouldn't have such a strong dislike for this genre if I hadn't been living in São Paulo during the time that 'Ai Se Eu Te Pego' came out. I don't feel like I'm exaggerating here when I say that this sertanejo song was overplayed to the point of nausea!

I remember hearing this song for the first time when I was with my friend, who turned to me and said, "You will hear this song so much now, especially during Carnival." He was right, but at the time he uttered these ominous words the song was new, it was fun and people were excited by the novelty of the accompanying dance routine (Note: Brazilians absolutely love their dance routines!).

Fast forward six months and this song was *still* being played excessively in bars and clubs, and people were *still* dancing to it like it was new. Whilst a lot of people I talked to were telling me that they were sick of hearing the song, it was almost like there was no escaping from it *anywhere* in São Paulo. I remember being in a club months after it came out, where the DJ was playing a variety of different kinds of music, including sertanejo. As soon as 'Ai Se Eu Te Pego' came on a load of people flocked to the dance floor to start dancing and a minute into the song my friend noticed me standing at the bar. He quickly stopped dancing to come over and see what was wrong. "Why are you not dancing to 'Ai Se Eu Te Pego'? Are you not having fun?"

There is nothing less fun than being asked by someone if you're having it.

"I don't really like this song, aren't you sick of it yet?" (I've made myself sound like such a good time on a night out!) In his drunken haze he appeared confused, almost like he couldn't understand why I'd grown to despise this song after only seven months of hearing it on a near-daily basis.

I have students who adore sertanejo and I even have friends who find it strange that I wouldn't want to go to one of these clubs with them to listen to it all night long. "But Andrew, what does 'thanks for the offer but I'd rather gauge my eyes out with a fork' mean?"

The Ugly – Funk Carioca

This style of music was born in the *favelas* (slums) of Rio, and is now very popular in many poor communities around Brazil. Personally I don't really mind this style of music. Admittedly its repetitive loops and samples grow tiresome after a while, but I don't find it all that unpleasant. Yet if you mention the words Funk Carioca to some Brazilians, you're likely to find that it evokes some strong negative feelings. It's definitely a Marmite style of music, with the majority of my female students turning their noses up at the genre whenever it gets mentioned. "Andrew, this music is so ugly and it portrays Brazilian woman in a way that is definitely not how we want the rest of the world to see us."

One gripe some have with this style is its use of vulgar lyrics. These have a reputation for being violent, sexually explicit and misogynistic. For example, in a lot of songs girls are referred to as *cachorras* (bitches) and *popozudas* (large asses). How delightful! And to think I used to find the blandness of my mum's *Best Of The Carpenters* album offensive!

Another issue some take with the style is the manner in which some women like to dance to it. I'll never forget the first time I saw anybody dancing to a Funk Carioca track; I was literally lost for words. I'd genuinely never seen anything quite like it before! On the same trip to Ubatuba I mentioned in the last chapter, I was sharing a house for the weekend with four guys and eight women. One evening someone plugged their iPod into some speakers and pumped out some loud music. As I walked inside to get a beer, this music switched from bubble gum pop to Funk Carioca. I walked outside with my beer to see that the majority of these women were dancing obscenely! They had their asses a few inches off the ground and were thrusting their crotches quite aggressively and contorting their bodies in time to the music. It was like something out of a banned rap video.

I think it was the sheer shamelessness of their dancing that struck me as being very different to what I was used to. They just looked so comfortable like this, gyrating in a way that I'm sure would even make Rihanna blush. I'm from England (the country that gave the world Jane Austen) and I've never seen women dancing like this there. If you'd like to know exactly what sort of dancing I'm talking about, a quick search on Youtube will bring up plenty of videos for you to watch (any of the Bonde das Maravilhas videos will definitely highlight what I mean!). Remember, you cannot un-see these. Also, I cannot be held personally responsible for recommending these videos to you if you're using your computer at work!

I can see why Funk Carioca has a bit of a bad name, yet it would be all too easy to write it off as simply being ugly and degrading. It is a genre of music that gives a voice to the underclass. Amongst other subjects of importance to *favela* communities, its lyrics deal with racial pride, social injustice and poverty.

So there you have it, my take on Brazilian music. I just wish I'd taken the time to enlighten myself on it a whole lot earlier; it would have prevented yet another awkward classroom moment for me!

Chapter Six – Five Things About Brazilians I Didn't Expect To Discover In My First Six Months

After living in São Paulo for almost six months I began to feel like I was getting used to both the city and its culture. For example, I knew it was a given that I would need to kiss a lot more than I was used to, that I'd be squashed into the metro during rush hour and that I could expect a 'BJ' at the end of most of my text messages from Brazilian women (Over here this is short for *beijo*, which means 'kiss' in Portuguese. For those Brazilians reading this, I'm pointing this out because in English a BJ refers to something *completely* different!). However every once in a while something happened that would serve as a reminder that I still had a lot to learn about Brazilian culture.

What's My Name?

Let me set the scene: I'd just ordered a cappuccino from Starbucks (I was really living the dream on a rainy Tuesday afternoon) and the woman behind the counter was holding her pen ready to write my name on a paper cup.

"Qual é o seu nome?" she asked me, chewing the hell out of her gum. She looked bored. Really bored. She was built like a cigarette box and she was giving off *a lot* of attitude.

I smiled at her and politely said, "Andrew!"

"Boom!" I thought, "those Portuguese classes are really starting to pay off."

There was a pause followed by a grunt.

"Eh?"

I repeated my name, this time a little louder and a little slower. "And-drew." She looked visibly bothered; in fact she looked like she wanted to smash my face in. I sensed she didn't know how to write 'Andrew'.

"Ehhhh?" she repeated, only this time her face was *really* screwed up, she was clearly irritated and she had even stopped chewing.

"Meu nome é A-N-DE-RE-W," I said, inadvertently sounding like I was giving her some attitude back. She glared at me. If looks could kill I'd be a dead man right now. She made no attempt to hide her irritation. Then she sighed heavily, shrugged her shoulders, chewed her gum again and then wrote my name down on the cup.

After she'd given me my change and receipt I sat down and waited. A good few minutes later the scrawny woman making drinks began to shout out a name.
"Alluhandraou."

Nobody stepped forward to claim the drink.

She repeated herself, "Alluhandraou."

"Alluhandraou."

Still nothing.

"Alluhandraou, Alluhandraou."

Those people who'd gone to Starbucks to chill out and read their books were getting visibly annoyed, as this woman continued to shout the same name. She did it with this weird diction that made her sound like she was fighting back a hairball.

Then it suddenly dawned on me. "Alluhandraou" could be me! I went up to check and when I got to the counter this scrawny woman shot me a filthy look, put my cappuccino down, turned around and walked off (presumably to bitch about me to the brick-shit-house on the till!).

I was Alluhandraou!

I retreated back to my seat and made sure to avoid eye contact with all the irked book readers. Then with my cappuccino in hand, I looked at my cup and noticed that woman had simply made up my name. To be fair to them, I am foreign. Foreign people sometimes have unusual sounding names; I just hadn't expected that mine was one of them. I thought this was odd because I hadn't had problems with Brazilians understanding my name before. But to prevent this from happening again, after discussing the incident with my Brazilian friends, we decided that from that moment on my Starbucks name should be a Brazilian one, Andre.

Brazilian Tooth Fairies

"Andrew, my nephew lost his first tooth yesterday!" my friend proudly announced after finishing a phone call to his family. "Aaaaaaaaawww!" I replied. "I bet he's excited to put it under his pillow tonight."

"His pillow? Andrew, why would he want to put his tooth under his pillow?"

"Well, for the tooth fairies," I said. I was surprised. I mean, how could my friend have forgotten about the tooth fairies already? He was still in his early twenties.

A silence followed.

"What is a tooth fairy?"

I was stunned; I'd assumed that the tooth fairies were universal. I then began to explain. "A tooth fairy is a small, erm, person with wings. They come into your room when you're sleeping, climb under your pillow and then swap your old tooth for money!"

He looked at me like I was winding him up. I could see a mixture of surprise and concern in his face as he went on to ask, "So in England small people with money fly into your bedroom and swap money for your tits? Seriously?"

Of course, I knew that he had meant to say 'teeth', not 'tits' (Thinking about it, I have no idea what purpose a tit fairy would serve!). So I found myself answering in the affirmative that the tooth fairy story was indeed true. Then I learnt that, without the help of tooth fairies to ensure kids grow up into materialistic adults, in Brazil children either throw their baby teeth out of their window, throw them up onto the roofs of their homes, put them under their beds or simply give them to their parents to keep (although parents over here have discovered tooth fairies through films or the Internet, and they are slowly being introduced here). With the help of Google I've been surprised to discover that loads of other countries don't have the tooth fairies either.

Who'd have thought!

Funerals

So this next example is pretty morbid but quite interesting at the same time. One evening my Facebook browsing was interrupted by a text message I'd received from a student. It read like this:

Andrew, I'm sorry, but I need to cancel our class tomorrow. My neighbour died today, so I need to go to the funeral. Bjs.

My first reaction was to write to let my student know how sorry I was to hear her sad news, but midway through this message I stopped. *Hang on a minute*, why was she going to a funeral just 24 hours after someone had died? I thought either this person's family is really keen to get this guy six feet under, or my student had simply come up with an elaborate story to get out of class.

Well, I later learnt Brazilians tend to bury their dead within 24 hours. With the weather being so hot and morgues not being very common out here, I can see why they would want to bury a body as soon as possible. I am aware that for some religions burying a body in this short time frame is common practice. Yet I'd assumed because Brazil is a Christian country like my own, they too would have the funeral a week or so later. Well, I was wrong.

A few days after receiving this text message I quizzed another of my students on the subject. "So what happens if a family member dies and you're, I don't know, you're abroad on holiday?" My student looked a little confused. Perhaps she was wondering what this question had to do with the previous one I'd asked on the subject of finance. But with a little hesitation she replied, "then you would miss the funeral."

If a member of my family died tomorrow I guess I take for granted that I'd have a few days to organise my trip back home for the funeral. If I was a Brazilian though, it's highly unlikely that I would be given this opportunity. I find this incredibly interesting.

Before this chapter becomes too morbid though, let's move on to ...

Pictures

"Excuse me, can you take my picture?" a solitary Brazilian woman asked when I was in Rio. Before I'd had the chance to oblige I'd been handed a camera and instructed on the direction in which I should point it.

"It's that big button on top," the woman smiled optimistically.

"Alright," I said, now focusing on the little screen in front of me. "In three …"

After hearing the beginning of the countdown, she turned her body to a 45 degree angle and tossed her long, brown locks over her left shoulder.

"Two."

A hand was placed on her hip, showcasing five perfectly polished and preened nails.

"One."

Her lips were then pursed into one hell of a pout.

FLASH!

After taking the picture I showed it to her and she studied it for a while. "No, can you take another one?" (I've learnt that Brazilian women are never very pleased with the first picture taken of them and will usually ask for a second.)

The reason I found this so intriguing was because the women I know back home wouldn't ask someone to take their picture, then pose as if they're on a shoot for *America's Next Top Model*. In comparison, British women are generally a lot more inhibited when it comes to having a camera in their faces, a little more awkward. Brits would probably only ask a stranger for another picture if they'd blinked or unwittingly displayed an epic-sized double chin, and even then they definitely wouldn't channel their inner Gisele for the shot. But women over here seem much more comfortable with having their picture taken – they really go for it!

Ali G Impersonations

In my time here I've found that Brazilians are pretty expressive. If they're not hugging or kissing you then they're punctuating what they're saying with plenty of gestures. For example, if you ask any Brazilian to tell you about a time they were in a crowded place, it has been scientifically proven that they will be unable to do so without turning their palms up, squeezing their fingers together, relaxing them for a moment and then squeezing them together again. "It was just so busy," they will tell you (mid crab impersonation!).

My favourite Brazilian gesture is not this one though; it is one Ali G made popular in the UK back in the '90's. When he was pleased about something he used to hold his thumb and middle finger together and whip his index finger back and forth to make a clicking noise. "Respect," he'd say, usually against the backdrop of a laughter track.

When people grew tired of the Ali G character this finger-clicking fad died out. But it was never an Ali G thing over in Brazil. I was once in a Portuguese class and I surprised myself by being able to bust out one of the complicated sentence structures I'd been practising the week before. "Yes Andrew," encouraged my elderly teacher, "Yes!" And to show just how pleased he was, he whipped his fingers back and forth.

I was as mesmerised by what I was seeing as I was impressed. You see, I can't do it. When I try it sometimes happens, but I can't do it on cue. Not like a Brazilian can. And when I say 'a Brazilian' I am deliberately including *all* Brazilians here. Male, female, young and old; I have yet to meet a Brazilian who can't do it!

Chapter Seven – Brazilian Women

    "So how are you finding living in Brazil?" asked a friend when I was visiting the UK to sort out my visa. As I began to reel off a stimulating response, "the fruit there is so cheap, as for the weather …" I was cut off with a real sense of urgency.

"Nice. Tell me about the women. They're all gorgeous out there, aren't they?" As soon as he'd asked, I saw a predatory smirk settling across his lips. It was pretty clear that I didn't need to reply; I could see he'd already made up his mind about Brazilian women and was merely affirming his opinion of them in my presence.

So I humoured him and asked what he thought they *all* looked like, and that's when he predictably began to describe beautiful women on the beaches in their tiny bikinis and scantily clad women dancing on top of carnival floats. I mean, of course he did! Every year during Carnival these images make their way into the British media, perpetuating the idea that woman here are all exotic goddesses.

And sure, there are a lot of beautiful women here, probably more so than in any of the other countries I've been to. But are they *all* beautiful? Christ no! These beautiful women I've mentioned are definitely not the only type of woman you will find in Brazil. For every scantily clad Carnival queen whose picture you see in the newspaper, there are so many who escape the photographer's lens. I'm talking specifically about the forgotten Brazilians now. The ugly ones!

"Andrew, there is no such thing as an ugly woman in Brazil … just a poor one!" joked a student once. This wasn't the first time I'd heard this link between beauty and wealth. In fact, when I invite Brazilian friends to free events in the city I often hear things like the following:

"I'd rather pay to go somewhere, feel safe and be around beautiful people than go somewhere free with poor, ugly people who will want to rob you." This idea took me some time to understand. In Brazil money not only buys decent clothes, haircuts and dental work (as in all countries), but it also gives you access to cosmetic surgery. And with the exception of America, Brazil is the world's largest consumer of it.

I used to give an evening class to three students, and as soon as our class had started I was told that one of these students was in a meeting and would be late. Twenty minutes into the class the door was thrown open and this student appeared in the doorway. She was sporting two black eyes and a nose wrapped in bandages. To say that she looked like she'd had a rough day would have been a bit of an understatement!

"Are you OK?" I enquired, sounding suitably concerned.

"Yes," she responded proudly as she took her seat. "I'm just recovering from my nose surgery." Far from being embarrassed about having it in the first place, she seemed to revel in the attention it brought her from the other students. A few weeks later those bandages were taken off, the swelling around the eyes had gone down and that nose was now more petite, which seemed to do wonders for her self-confidence.

I've been told that there isn't much of a stigma about going under the surgeon's knife in Brazil, that it's a status thing. "Well, if you can afford it, why would you keep it a secret?" one of my Brazilian friends asked me when discussing the subject. "But then again," she continued, "everyone seems to be having it done nowadays. You can even get it done for free in some clinics, so it's really not a big deal anymore."

In the UK women are much more discreet about surgical work they've had done, as if admitting to having a surgeon tampering with their looks in their quest for beauty somehow makes them less of a woman. Well, interestingly, the opposite seems to be true here.

What do Brazilian women actually look like anyway?

A few years ago I was at a house party where I was introduced to a friend of a friend. After she'd discovered I was from the UK she was quite keen to tell me about the time she'd spent studying in London. The conversation meandered from places she'd visited, to British culture and then on to the indie bands she was fond of.

"I love Alt-J," she said with such a contagious enthusiasm that I found myself declaring my love for them too, despite having never heard of them. The mood then became a little more serious as she explained that there was one thing she found strange about the time she'd spent living in the UK. "People were often surprised when I told them that I was Brazilian. 'But you're so pale!' they used to say. One guy even made me show him my passport to prove I wasn't lying. He thought I looked too white to be Brazilian."

As I looked at her again, the one thing that struck me about her was that she really didn't look like those images of Brazilian woman we see back home. In fact, her dyed black hair accentuated the marble whiteness of her skin to such an extent … she looked more Morticia Addams than she did carnival queen.

"Really? They didn't believe you?" I sighed.

"That's right," she confirmed. "It's true." Finding I'd done right with my first sigh I did it again, which encouraged her to elaborate. "I suppose I just don't look Brazilian to some people abroad."

This conversation got me thinking: it is such a shame people challenged her on whether she was really Brazilian or not. One thing I appreciate about living here is that the country is so multicultural. It doesn't really have a single ethnic identity because it is made up of a mixture of so many different races.

To hear that my fellow Brits hadn't realised this when they were questioning her identity was disappointing. But then, before coming here I too assumed women would adhere to the stereotypical image the world is frequently offered. So is it entirely our fault that some of us think like this?

No, I really don't think it is. Especially when you consider that sometimes even Brazilians have trouble picking out other Brazilians from a crowd. According to one of my Brazilian students of Japanese heritage, in Rio she often encounters locals who assume she's not Brazilian. "Andrew, whenever I go there I have so many *Cariocas* (people from Rio) trying to charge me extra for things because they think I'm foreign. But then to them I guess I don't look Brazilian, I look Japanese. Not many Brazilians of Japanese descent live in Rio."

This really baffled me because the city of São Paulo is home to the largest population of Japanese outside of Japan, and São Paulo is about a six-hour bus journey away from Rio. Yet the Japanese community really isn't very prevalent over in Rio. But when you look at where immigrants have settled throughout Brazil, they haven't spread evenly throughout the country. For example, large communities of Brazilians of African descent can be found towards the north of the country, Brazilians of German descent tend to gravitate towards the south and there are also (to name just a few) pockets of Italians, Portuguese and Bolivians scattered around Brazil too.

So with such an array of ethnicities dotted around the country, it goes without saying that women in Brazil are going to look different depending on where in the country you are. I've even heard about another difference between the Brazilians in different regions that I'd not really given too much thought to until a few years ago: their height.

Tall Brazilian Women

I was attending my friend's wedding once when I got talking to a tall, beautiful woman with long, dyed-blonde locks. After asking her where she worked she told me that she spent most of her time in the city of Manaus (in the north east of Brazil). After a few drinks this conversation took an unprompted (and slightly unexpected) turn into her Bridget Jones-esque love life.

"I've been single for so long, and I'm not really in São Paulo long enough to be involved with anyone here. But, of course, there's little chance of me meeting a guy in Manaus. I'm seen as a bit of a freak over there." At this she tossed her hair over her left shoulder and looked down at the floor, obviously waiting for me to enquire a little further.

I didn't get it, why would this attractive, tall Brazilian woman find it difficult to find a man to date in the north of the country? Was she looking down at her webbed feet? Intrigued, I naturally dug a little deeper in the most eloquent way I could.

"Eeeeeer … what do you mean?"

"Well," she began, "it's because I'm so much taller than the majority of the women up there. In fact, the guys in the office have a nickname for me because of my height." She then paused to look at me with eyes I'd seen once before, on a wounded puppy during the TV show *Animal Hospital*.

Her voice lowered. "They call me … the Avatar."

I felt really bad for laughing at this comment as soon as she'd said it. In an attempt to redeem myself I immediately managed a serious expression that I felt helped me look a little more sympathetic.

"They don't, do they?" I asked, sounding disappointed (with only a hint of amusement still audible in my voice).

"Yes, 'the big Avatar from São Paulo' is my nickname. So it's easier for me to find someone here where I'm not seen as being freakishly tall." I'd not had many dealings with people from the north east of Brazil so I hadn't really thought of them as being any smaller than people from the rest of the country. But apparently there is a difference.

Brazilian Mamas

A chapter on women wouldn't be complete without discussing the importance of the Brazilian mother to most Brazilians. Getting my friends to go out the Saturday night before Mother's Day is almost impossible, because very few on this sacred day would dare greet the family matriarch with a hangover. When it comes to the Brazilian Mama you should do your best not to get on the wrong side of one, as I unwittingly almost did when I travelled to my friend's home city of Sorocaba: the eighth biggest city in the state of São Paulo.

During our night out, I unwisely overindulged in the overpriced *caipirinha*-slushies. The next morning I awoke, not just to an empty wallet and a pounding headache, but also to a surprise family dinner to celebrate Carlos' birthday. When I say a family dinner, I mean an army of family members had descended on Carlos' house to mark the occasion with a feast. With many mouths to feed this was a feast that was demolished very quickly! After a few hours of sitting round trying to understand what people were talking about in Portuguese, it was time for my friends and I to head back to São Paulo.

Because we were all taking the same bus back with Carlos, we ended up being the last guests to leave. Just as we were about ready to go I found myself alone in the kitchen with Carlos' mother. Being the absolute British gent that I am, I took this opportunity to thank her for her hospitality. I'd just started to speak when she grabbed a two litre bottle out of the fridge and interrupted me. "Would you like a bottle of my acerola juice?" she asked in Portuguese. She looked so enthusiastic about this juice that I actually felt bad about saying no.

As much as I'd have loved to have accepted, the main reason I declined was not that I'd never heard of an acerola before (also known as a Barbados cherry ... yea, me neither!), but that I'd already brought a backpack full of things with me. There was no way I'd have been able to ram a bottle that big into my bag without the zips giving way. Surprisingly, her face maintained its enthusiasm at this refusal. When I attempted to continue and again thank her for letting me crash at her house, she raised this bottle a little closer to me and interrupted, repeating her original question.

"Would you like a bottle of my acerola juice?"

The thought of lugging this bottle into a taxi, onto a bus and then onto the metro was just too much for my pulsating head to deal with at this point. So again I declined her offer, except this time I was a little firmer.

"No, but thank you *very* much for offering."

She continued to stare at me whilst clutching this bottle. I don't remember seeing her blink once. After an awkward few seconds she repeated her question, seemingly undeterred by my other refusals.

"This can be your acerola juice if you like?" she pleaded, having shaped her question differently for me. At that my friend walked into the kitchen and was immediately collared by his mum. "Carlos," she began, as if the thought had just occurred to her that maybe I hadn't understood what she'd been asking in Portuguese, despite us only communicating in Portuguese, "ask Andrew if he wants some of my acerola juice."

"Andrew, my mama wants to know if you'd like some of her acerola juice."

"Carlos, please tell your mum I said thank you, but ..."

"What are you doing? My mama makes really good acerola juice!" He said this in a way that not only suggested he was incredibly surprised I wouldn't want this bloody big bottle of a juice I'd never heard of, but also that I was offending him personally by not taking it.

Now, as a Brit I'm fairly well versed in the habit of being polite. I'd been very firm but friendly and had even thanked his mum for her offer. So I was at a bit of loss as to what I was supposed to do now without sounding rude. "My mama loves to give food and drink to people who come to our house, Andrew. She will be really disappointed if you don't take the bottle. We have an acerola tree in the garden, you know."

Well, the last thing I wanted to do was upset his mother; she'd put me up for the night and had welcomed me and our friends around her family dinner table. I just didn't want this bottle of friggin acerola juice! However, I soon conceded that there was no getting around it. That bottle had had my name written all over it right from the start!

"So, does he want some acerola juice, Carlos?" she asked again. I've got to hand it to my friend's mother: she is incredibly persistent.

"Yes, Andrew," Carlos repeated whilst looking intently at me, "would you like some of my mama's *really good* acerola juice?"

"Erm, yes," I said, "I would!"

A huge grin spread across Carlos' mum's face as she announced that she would put it in a bag for me. Seconds later I was the proud owner of this large bottle, and my other friends left the house with their own life sized bottles of acerola juice too. We all spent the next two hours dragging them home. As it turns out my friend was right, his 'mama' really does make great juice. But I'm not writing about this incident just to tell you this. My reason for sharing this story is to pass on what I learned from this day.

If you're offered food or drink by a Brazilian Mama and you have a feeling that she might not take 'no' for an answer, it's wise for you to just accept whatever is being offered. Even if it's the last thing you actually want. "When I go to certain people's houses," recalled one of my students, "I know I'm going to be offered a lot of food and I will feel bad if I refuse it. But there are some housewives in Brazil who love nothing more than feeding their guests, again and again and again!"

When I posted about this incident on my blog, one reader wrote to share a similar story with me. A few weeks into moving to Brazil he was staying with his mother-in-law and she offered him a *coxinha* (a traditional food in Brazil), but because he was on a diet he politely declined. However, in doing so his mother-in-law was so put out by this refusal that she refused to talk to him for the rest of the day!

Not all Brazilian mothers (and, of course, grandmothers) are like this, but coming from the UK where things are frequently offered out of courtesy or politeness (for example, I *never* want someone to accept when I offer out my chocolate, but feel I have to ask before I can fully enjoy it), someone being so assertive when they offer you food and drink is something I'm still getting used to.

Chapter Eight – Crime

In my second year here, after almost ten consecutive months of living amongst the chaos of São Paulo, I decided that the time had come to take a break from the city. So I booked a trip to Florianopolis with the sole intention of slobbing out on the beaches, bronzing my lily-white body and experiencing some of the city's nightlife.

As the sun set on my first full day at the beach I dragged my lobster-red body back to my hostel with a loose plan of hitting up one of the city's nightclubs that evening. After consulting Google Maps I noticed that I could take a bus that would drop me a few blocks away from the club I wanted to go to. So I scribbled down the address on some paper, showered, slept a little, showered again and then took the last bus into the city centre.

As I stepped off the bus I immediately noticed that, despite it being a Saturday night, the main street was eerily deserted. There were very few people around and nowhere looked to be open, which immediately struck me as being odd. Then out of the corner of my eye I spotted a group of about six policemen stood around talking. So I wandered over to get some directions from them.

"*Desculpa*," (Sorry) I said, whilst clumsily unfolding my notepaper with the address written on it. I was about to bust out my caveman-like Portuguese when a young-looking policeman stepped forward.

"Can I help you?" he asked in near-perfect English.

"Erm, yes," I said, a little taken aback. I'd not encountered too many Brazilian policemen speaking English before. "Can you tell me where this nightclub is?" I enquired, passing the paper over to him. After momentarily glancing at it he nodded. "Sure, you'll need to walk straight up this street and it will be on your left." As he said this he gestured up a narrow, dimly lit street that looked like something you'd expect to see in a low budget horror film. It was a little too dark and a little too empty for my liking.

"Erm … is it safe? I won't get robbed, will I?" I asked. To my surprise, the police officer made no attempt to disguise the fact he thought this was funny.

"Gringo," he laughed, before tilting his head to one side and talking to me as if I were a slow-learning puppy. "*Nowhere* in Brazil is safe; so good luck walking up there!"

As he turned his back on me to rejoin his colleagues I heard him relaying a translated version of our conversation to them. I took this as my cue to leave, and after just a couple of strides up Elm Street this group of policemen all let out knowing, hearty laughs. These laughs rang in my ears for the few minutes it took me to power walk up this street.

It was only when I was safely inside the venue that I felt relaxed enough to process what had just happened. Of course, I hadn't expected an officer to escort me up the street, but I certainly hadn't expected this group of law enforcers to have found my question quite as amusing as they had. Especially as I was asking about my safety on the streets they were patrolling!

This brings me on to one aspect of life in Brazil that I'm sure everyone living in the city has at least thought about:

Getting Robbed

Before I begin, I think it is worth pointing out that what I write here is a personal reflection of my own experiences of living in São Paulo, coupled with experiences of those around me. Maybe you live in this city, or have visited, and you can identify with the experiences I'm about to describe. Or perhaps you will disagree with what I write partially, or even completely, because your time here is, or has been, affected by crime in a much more significant way than my own. But I think as every resident of São Paulo will agree, the threat of being robbed in this city is very real.

This was brought home to me just a few weeks into starting my teaching position. One evening a female student walked into class looking noticeably distressed, and as she sat down a fellow student asked her if she was feeling alright. This prompted her to recall what had happened to her earlier that day. So at seven that morning she'd been walking to the bus stop when a guy had pulled a gun out on her, demanding she hand over her valuables.

I remember sitting open mouthed as she told us this; I couldn't believe it.

Then one of her colleagues made this remark. "Seven? Wow! They're getting up early, aren't they!?!"

It took me a few seconds to consider what he'd just said. I was shocked that my student had been robbed in the first place, and there he was making observations about the early hour in which the incident had taken place.

We were clearly not on the same page!

Since this conversation it would be no exaggeration to say that I'm now hearing stories like this on a weekly basis. Perhaps what I'm about to say is going to sound cold, but I feel like I am becoming desensitised to hearing about this sort of thing now. I hadn't realised this was the case until after a year or so of being here, when my friend told me that he had been robbed on the subway. Someone had gone into his backpack and taken out his credit cards and documents. He'd only noticed when he got to work and found that his bag had been opened.

"Well, why would you put your stuff in the front of your backpack? That's just asking for trouble," I asserted dismissively, as if he bore some of the blame for what happened to him. I'm not usually an unsympathetic person (despite what my ex might tell you!) but I guess I've hardened to hearing about this sort of thing now.

On reflection it's almost as if I don't recognise my earlier, overcautious attitude. If I'm being honest the threat of crime intimidated me in my first few months here and I was constantly looking over my shoulder. This feeling stayed with me for a loooooong time.

Fast forward to today though and I've become much more laid back about the possibility that I may get robbed. Having heard plenty of first-hand accounts from my students, I've almost accepted that it is inevitable at some point it will probably happen to me too. And recognising this was somewhat of a revelation because, instead of constantly worrying about it, I now just get on with living here. Don't get me wrong: I'm still cautious, just not in a way that's as consuming as it once was. In a word I've adapted. The threat of being robbed isn't something I think of as being such a big deal any more. It is just there.

During one insightful conversation I had on the subject of crime in Brazil with a student, I was given some advice on what to do if I were to become the victim of a robbery on the street. Since hearing it, it's occupied a place in my thoughts ever since:

"I recently read an article in a magazine about robbery," my student began, "where the journalists interviewed thieves who'd actually killed their victims. They'd murdered these people because they had refused to hand over their belongings, or because they'd put up a fight. These criminals had said that the moment they'd decided to threaten someone with a gun or a knife was when they felt they had the most power. So to be told 'no' or to have had someone resisting handing over their things, well, this was when the knife had been used or the trigger had been pulled."

"Andrew, these people often don't respect their own lives, so it's too much to ask that they're going to respect yours too. Some of these guys have nothing to lose. If you get robbed just hand over your things; valuables can easily be replaced."

This attitude was quite alien to me at first. "But they are *my* things, I would want to keep them," I remember thinking. But very few people have advised me to fight back; it just doesn't seem worth it.

Having said this, there are a few things that you can do to minimise the risk of being in this situation in the first place. Here is a summary of what I consider to be the best pieces of advice I've been given during my time here. I've focused this list on São Paulo, but a lot of what I'm about to write could also be applied to other cities in Brazil. So without further ado, here goes:

Tip #1

Don't walk around with your valuables on display. Parading around with the sort of expensive laptops, phones and jewellery that poorer residents of the city can't afford is simply not a good idea. Some may even see it as being disrespectful. I mean, you wouldn't wear Lady Gaga's meat dress if you had to go into a lion's den around feeding time and then expect nothing to happen to you, would you? Hell no!

My advice would be to either hide these things away when in public places, or, better still, leave them at home/in your hotel. Walking around the city with the latest equipment in full view could make you a target for opportunist thieves, so be discreet.

Tip #2

Avoid walking around the centre of the city at night, as you might unwittingly be leaving yourself vulnerable to theft. This area is notorious for its crack addicts, and certain parts are definitely best to be avoided.

Tip #3

Don't carry large amounts of cash on you, but at the same time try to make sure you have a little to hand over should you find yourself the victim of a robbery. If someone wants money from you and you have nothing, you could be in trouble. Aim to have at least 20 reals in your pocket.

Tip #4

Secure your valuables before getting onto crowded trains or metros, particularly during rush hour. With all of those bodies pressed tightly up against each other, you might not even feel São Paulo's answer to Fagin removing something from your pocket or bag.

Tip #5

Whenever using cars/taxis, keep your valuables out of view of passing motorbikes. Unfortunately if you are stuck in traffic, there is a risk that someone on a motorbike may take a fancy to what they see through the car window (which is why many vehicles here have windows blacked out). If you're sandwiched between cars, thieves are going to be able to make a quick and easy getaway with your things. So place valuables under the seat of your car, or, better still, lock them away in the boot.

If you're driving in São Paulo at night it is also worth noting that traffic lights are to be seen as a guide. If you can see that there is nothing coming when you're at a crossroads, it is advisable to continue on with your journey, sounding your horn as you go. You don't want to be sitting stationary unnecessarily, what with cars being an easy target in quiet areas at night.

Of course, there is no surefire way to avoid being robbed, but being aware of how significant the risk is here will allow you to think accordingly, and hopefully will also ensure you have a safe stay in Brazil.

Is Brazil as dangerous as people say it is?

Reading this chapter back I'm aware that I've made São Paulo sound like something from a game of *Grand Theft Auto*. And perhaps I'm being unintentionally controversial as I write this, but the São Paulo I know isn't actually that bad. In fact, when I was back in England I was astonished when my friend asked me if I'd ever seen a shoot-out in the streets.

"A shoot-out?" I repeated. "Erm no, never." He looked quite sceptical at my response, as if I wasn't telling him the whole truth. This is when I wondered what some people actually think about my life over here. I mean, I'm more than happy for them to think I'm some sort of badass adrenalin junkie playing down the fact I'm often dodging bullets and fists on my way to the grocery store. The truth is this is simply not the case at all (well, the part about me dodging bullets and fists isn't, but the part about me being a total badass is *obviously* completely true!). Not only have I never seen a shoot-out, I've also never seen anyone being robbed. In addition I've seen less than a handful of fights in the whole time I've been here.

But some have these assumptions about Brazil, and from my own experience of being brought up in the UK I guess I can understand why. Prior to my first trip here the only exposure I'd had of the country was through news reports, and, with the exception of those reports focused on Carnival celebrations and football, the majority featured crime. Then there are films like *City Of God* and *The Elite Squad* which, despite being great films, again focus on the darker side of life in Brazil. So you could easily forgive some for assuming life here is reminiscent of a Tarantino film. Yet my experience of living in São Paulo hasn't been like this at all.

I know that there are people here living in neighbourhoods a lot more dangerous than my own, whose lives are affected by crime in a much more significant way. My intention is not to undermine or to dismiss how prevalent crime is for these people, but to point out that my time here hasn't been reflected by the worst aspects of life in Brazil shown in the international media.

I think it's important to point this out because there are often people coming to the city through work or whatever, worried that the whole city is a large den of opportunist thieves and trigger-happy gun users.

On one hand I know São Paulo is a big city with depravity, crime and poverty; yet on the other, the areas I spend most of my time don't really feel any less safe than places I've been to in London. And the riots there in 2011 went some way to highlight that London is no safe haven either. I was visiting the north of England at the time the riots took place, watching them unfold through the safety of my TV set. Like the majority of the country at the time, I couldn't get my head around the fact people were destroying their own communities. Yet because I wasn't living in the area directly affected by the riots I dismissed it as being 'a southern thing'. I saw it as something that didn't really affect me because I wasn't in the south of the country.

And similarly whenever I see crime scenes reported on the news channels here in São Paulo, I think, "Ah, that's in the centre of the city, well, that doesn't really affect me because I don't live there." But I appreciate that there will be people abroad who care little for the geography of the city, who are likely to assume that the crime reports they've seen in specific areas of São Paulo are reflective of life throughout the entire city.

I was certainly guilty of thinking like that when a student told me about how he'd enjoyed his second holiday in as many years to Mexico City. After he'd told me where he'd been I sat in a reflective silence for a while.

"But did you feel safe there?"

"Andrew, Mexico City is huge and despite what you may have read, it's not that bad. I wouldn't have gone there on holiday again if it was."

I was momentarily stuck for something to say. I couldn't really argue with that!

When São Paulo Feels Safer Than Places In The UK

You might be surprised to hear that there is one aspect of life here that trumps the UK in terms of personal safety and this is related to alcohol consumption. During the first Carnival I ever spent in São Paulo I found myself in the midst of a wild street party. Carnival-goers had packed the streets to enjoy the live music, the sunshine and the ice cold beer being sold by vendors on street corners. These parties (known as *blocos*) are a big part of Carnival celebrations and are a whole lot of fun.

I noticed that the parties had a surprisingly low police presence for the large amount of people filling the streets. As it turned out, a lot of police weren't needed. With most of the people at these parties out to dance, drink and enjoy themselves, the atmosphere was both electric and (perhaps more importantly) it felt safe.

"Do you have parties in the UK like this?" asked my friend as we followed the truck blasting out live samba music down the street.

"Well, no, not really," I replied. "British people tend to fight a lot when they're drunk, which is probably why drinking on the street is illegal there."

He looked at me with the same expression I once saw my sister pulling when she'd worked out the plot twist at the end of *The Sixth Sense*.

"Illegal? Really? But why do many people in England fight after drinking beer?"

At that I shrugged my shoulders because I really didn't have an answer. Maybe I'm being unfair as I write this but I suspect carnival celebrations without a huge police presence wouldn't work in the UK. Often Brits + Beer = Fights.

Of course, I'm not saying there are no alcohol-related fights in Brazil, because there are. Yet in comparison with what I was used to seeing in the UK, I really haven't seen that many. I would even go as far as to say that I feel much safer amongst a crowd of drunken Brazilians than I do a crowd of drunken Brits. Brazil may have its problems when it comes to crime and danger; but if you exercise an air of caution when you're over here you're likely to find your relationship with crime isn't going to be a significant one, despite what the international media may have you believe

Chapter Nine – Football

Anybody who knows me personally is probably going to be surprised that I've devoted an entire chapter of this book to the subject of football. You see, I'm not really what you'd call much of a fan of the 'beautiful game'. Having said this I know all the basics; for example, I can explain the offside rule and I get really involved in watching England's international matches too (for as long as the bar is open anyway!). As I'm teaching students who are incredibly passionate about football, there is literally no avoiding the subject in my classes. What this means is that I'm now surprisingly quite clued up on football here.

An Idiot's Guide To Football In São Paulo

When my football-loving students used to ask me what team I followed back home, I soon learnt not to answer with "erm, well, I don't really like football." When I said this I was able to read the look on their faces. It was a look that said 'I like talking to you, just not as much as I did ten seconds ago.'

Whenever I'm asked now I tell people I support Middlesbrough which is the nearest city to my hometown. This generally elicits a positive response because of its Brazilian connection. This city in the north of England was once home to the former Brazilian international, Juninho Paulista. When he arrived in Middlesbrough back in the mid-nineties, supporters were delighted that a club so small could attract a footballer of such great stature (I'm referring to his status as a World Cup winning player here and not his height. The guy is absolutely tiny!). Back then I used to wonder how Juninho was adapting to his new life amongst the smoke stacks and the cold weather of Middlesbrough. It seemed like a million miles away from the tropical Brazil I'd seen through my TV set.

Before playing on British soil the team Juninho used to belong to was São Paulo. This is just one of the three main clubs here in the city and not the main one as I'd originally assumed. I soon learnt that fans of São Paulo Football Club have a lot more teasing directed at them than any of these other clubs, and it took me some time to work out why.

São Paulo FC

Back when I was starting out as an English teacher, my students used to tell me who they supported in the hope they could convince me to adopt their team too. Whenever someone in my group classes told me that they supported São Paulo, the following would happen: the other students in my class would laugh, start shouting out 'Bambi' and then advise me never to support this team.

One day I asked one of my students why São Paulo supporters were constantly being teased. "Andrew," began my Palmeiras-loving student with a smirk, "they have the type of supporter who enjoys fine wines and novels." He allowed these words to linger in the air for a moment, as if to emphasise that he thought enjoying wine and books was a bad thing. As someone who majored in English Literature at university (and minored in drinking cheap wine), I like novels (and the odd glass of *vinho*). In fact, as soon as he said this to me I remember thinking that this football team sounded right up my street. Before I'd had the chance to think too much about getting myself a season ticket though, I was thrown a knowing look: "Do you know what I mean?"

My face must have given me away. I really didn't.

"I'll put it another way then … they are all Bambis!" He then laughed for a while until he realised I wasn't laughing along with him. It wasn't clear to me who Bambi was or what position he played in, but I could see that he was a major reason that supporters of the club were being mocked. I'd heard his name being thrown around *a lot* before this conversation too. Another student then came to my rescue: "He means they are all gay! We call São Paulo players and their supporters Bambis from the Disney movie, because they play football like gays!"

It had been a while since I last saw the film *Bambi*, but I really didn't remember this deer (who so tragically lost his mother) being homosexual. "Erm," I said out loud, "what does Bambi have to do with gay football players?"

Well, it turns out that because Bambi is considered effeminate, fans of other teams in the city enjoy using this nickname for supporters of São Paulo Football Club. "Andrew, you must remember how Bambi walked on ice? Well, this is how players from this team run when they play football." I've seen a few São Paulo games on TV now and I can confirm that this is, in fact, a big lie! They really don't run like Bambi skidding around on ice at all! I've since discovered that the deer is an animal generally associated with homosexuality in Brazil, which doesn't make a whole lot of sense to me. But the lesson I learnt from this conversation was the following: understanding Brazilian culture isn't always easy if you think too much about it; sometimes you just have to accept things at face value!

Corinthians vs. Palmeiras

The other two major teams with home grounds inside the city of São Paulo are Corinthians and Palmeiras. These two are huge rivals.

The story goes that about 100 years ago a London-based team called Corinthians toured Brazil and inspired a group of working-class Brazilian footballers to form their own team. Just ten days after the British Corinthians played in São Paulo, the São Paulo-Corinthians were playing their first match. This tedious link back to the UK is one I give to justify why I prefer Corinthians to Palmeiras. Of course, this is not the real reason at all. I've picked the team I support over here in much the same way I would pick a horse at the races. I prefer their name.

Interestingly Palmeiras were founded just a few years after Corinthians, and were formed to represent the Italian community in the city. Initially they were supported by fans of Italian descent, but nowadays their supporters include a much more diverse mix of people.

Other Nicknames

So, São Paulo's fans are known as Bambis, and Palmeiras fans get called *'porcos'* (pigs) by their rivals. I can't work out why their nickname is *'porcos'* and neither can anybody I've asked; their mascot is a green bird that doesn't look much like a pig at all. Corinthians are referred to as skunks because apparently they smell bad, and Santos' fans are simply nicknamed *'peixe'* (fish) because the city of Santos is by the sea. Football fans presumably weren't feeling nearly as creative when they came up with that nickname!

Santos

This brings me onto Neymar and Pele's former club of Santos FC. Despite the city of Santos being only 80 km away from São Paulo, I have met relatively few supporters of the club here. When I quizzed my students on why this was, they pointed out that after Pele left the club in the '70s the club's winning streak began to dry up. This meant that the next generation of football fans living in São Paulo became less enthusiastic about Santos and so they then began to follow other more exciting teams. As time went on these older Santos supporters became known as 'Pele's widows', guys who followed the club because of the time they'd invested in it during its glory days.

Football On TV

So, that's a pretty brief rundown on the clubs, but something else a foreigner coming over here might also find interesting is the time of night that football games are played. Over in my native UK, soap operas dominate the early evening TV fixtures. Premier League matches don't really affect these shows because games are generally played on Saturdays. Every once in a while, though, soap operas are replaced by live Champions League games.

"What is this I'm watching?" my mum asked on several occasions when I was growing up. As four football pundits sat in a studio debating an upcoming game, my mum would look noticeably irritated that Coronation Street had been taken off air. Like many soap lovers up and down the UK, she did not take kindly to this kind of disruption. She seemed to have this belief that if she pressed button number 3 hard enough, she could alter what the TV channel was broadcasting to the entire nation. But when football games clash with soap operas in the UK there is only ever going to be one winner.

I imagined the same would happen over here, what with Brazil being the country known for its love of the game. Intriguingly this isn't the case. I heard a rumour that Globo (the terrestrial TV channel that owns the rights to the major soaps) also owns the rights to the majority of Brazil's football games. So it made a deal with the clubs over here some time ago, and now games generally won't kick off until the *novelas* (the name given to soaps in Portuguese) final credits have finished rolling. It's actually quite normal for a football game to start around 9 or 10pm over here. This means fans of *novelas* aren't really affected by football, and TV channels won't miss out on the revenue TV advertisements bring in during soap operas. Everyone's a winner then, right? Well, yes ...

everyone, that is, except light sleepers.

Whenever Corinthians, Palmeiras or São Paulo are involved in a big match, it's a given that on the night these games are played (usually on Wednesdays or Sundays), fireworks will be exploding throughout the city and car horns will be honked with gusto. The residents of São Paulo like to express their passion for big games loudly! This is NOT what a sleep-loving killjoy like me wants to hear as I try to get some shut-eye, especially when I need to be up early for work the next morning.

Back in 2012, Corinthians played Boca Juniors in the Libertadores Cup Final. They'd never won this cup before so fans had been eagerly awaiting the game as soon as the team qualified for it. When I walked into my student's office at around 7pm on the night of this match, despite kick-off not being for a good few hours, fireworks had already been going off around the city for hours. An hour later when I was wrapping up my class, I asked my student if he was looking forward to the game. "Not really," he answered without hesitation. "I have an eleven-month-old baby at home who won't be able to sleep tonight because of the noise in this city. These fireworks mean tonight is going to be a very long night for us all."

With this game being such a big deal, my morning students had cancelled our class the next day so that they could enjoy the game over a few beers. This meant I had an empty schedule the next morning, and so I decided to join my friends to watch the match in our packed local bar. The first half wasn't particularly exciting, but during the second half things got interesting when Corinthians scored.
"Gooooooooooooooal," screamed the commentator against the backdrop of car horns and fireworks. When the referee blew the whistle to signal Corinthians had been victorious, the bar erupted in cheers. From this moment on fireworks began pounding against the night sky and I was still hearing them

right the way up to lunchtime the following day. Turns out a whole load of people wouldn't have been sleeping as soundly as they'd have liked this night!

Football Commentators

Let me get back to the one aspect of football here I find really bizarre, the way the commentators scream the word 'goal'. I'm sure they get trained at the Mariah Carey School of note-holding because they stretch this word out for an unnaturally long time. In fact, it wouldn't surprise me if these guys have contracts that ban them from smoking or if some participate in deep-sea diving on their days off. Their lung capacity must be huge. I mean, it has to be! They make British commentators seem very reserved in comparison, something that was once picked up on by a student:

 "I was in England watching a Manchester United game in a pub, and when they scored the commentator said the word 'goal' really quickly. He sounded so cold, like scoring a goal wasn't all that exciting!"

The three students listening to this were visibly intrigued, with one asking, "Andrew, is this true?" I realised that everyone was waiting for verbal confirmation, so I reluctantly told them that it was. "Well, yes, we do say it quite quickly. But, let's be honest, it's not really necessary to scream 'goal' as long as you can, is it?" I could see from the look on those faces that I was fighting a losing battle. When a Brazilian sees a goal being scored on TV, boy they expect to hear about it! First from an excessively enthusiastic commentator, and then in the form of the fireworks and car horns! Had Sleeping Beauty been living in São Paulo, I'm pretty sure she wouldn't have needed to have waited for her Prince Charming to wake her up, especially if she was sleeping near one of the main football stadiums!

Chapter Ten – Brazilian Beach Culture

I'm now going to discuss one aspect of living here I continue to find incredibly fascinating: Brazilian beach culture. It was during my first-ever visit to Copacabana beach that I became acquainted with it. As I stepped out onto the world-famous sandy beach, I looked around and was a little taken aback by what I saw. On this particular day there were women in tiny dental-floss bikinis and men sporting pretty tight Speedos (or *sunga* as they're known over here), parading their flesh as far down the beach as the eye could see. Almost everyone was just a slither of fabric or two away from being completely naked. I, on the other hand, had walked onto that beach looking fairly conservative in my white vest and knee-length board shorts (like a *Downton Abbey* extra!).

I really felt like I'd been summoned into another world, one in which I was incredibly overdressed. A few years later and I was *still* wearing this sort of clothing to the beach, despite knowing how different I looked to most of my Brazilian friends. But the voice inside my head was still screaming at me all these years later, telling me not to even think about wearing a Speedo!

In the UK there is stigma attached to wearing a pair; it's just competitive swimmers (and, of course, Tom Daley) who can really get away with wearing them. Some public pools have even banned guys from wearing the garment because, when you're around women and children, the lump and bump enhancing Speedo is considered pretty inappropriate. I know that many Europeans are also fond of wearing the item and that it isn't exclusive to Brazilians on the beach, but I was still interested to know why so many men feel comfortable wearing them here.

"Aren't you worried that everyone will be able to see … everything?" I asked my friend Carlos when discussing the Speedo he wears to the beach. As soon as these words came rolling off my tongue his face stretched out into a mocking grin, "Andrew. If people can see my dick through my *sunga* and don't like it, this isn't my problem, it's theirs! And why would they want to look anyway?"

This certainly sounds like a convincing argument. However, when you're relaxing on a reclining chair on the beach and suddenly the sunlight you've been enjoying becomes eclipsed by your friend's body, you instinctively look up to see what's going on. This is when you may well find yourself in the position I was once in, coming face to face with a less than subtle outline of your friend's genitals. Sometimes seeing them is just unavoidable around men in tight fabric.

When I asked some of my male students why they choose to wear a *sunga* on the beach, many looked at me in genuine confusion and asked, "Well, why wouldn't we wear a *sunga*?" I felt like I'd just asked them to explain something really obvious to me, like water. Lesson learnt: for some Brazilians the Speedo is just staple beachwear.

Interestingly, some of my Brazilian blog readers living outside of São Paulo have assured me that they don't care too much for *sungas*. One from Florianopolis wrote to tell me that he always wears board shorts at the beach, yet in contrast another from Rio told me that he wouldn't be seen dead in a pair of shorts (they are synonymous with how the lower classes dress on the beach there). So the Speedo isn't a nationwide phenomenon.

As much as I tried to justify to myself why I shouldn't wear a Speedo, my reluctance to don a pair was often met with smirks from my friends. "Oh look, Andrew is still wearing his foreigner shorts," said one quite patronisingly at the beach a few years ago. The trouble is, when you are the only one *not* wearing a Speedo it's difficult to argue that you're the one who doesn't look ridiculous. So, after almost four years here, one afternoon I impulsively decided to bite the bullet and just go for it. I was walking along the beach in Rio and spotted a guy with a makeshift swimwear stand. I wandered over, pointed out a pair of dark blue trunks (the type that Daniel Craig can pull off. If it's good enough for Bond then it's definitely good enough for me!), and two minutes later I was a member of this elusive Speedo owners club!

I knew that buying a pair would be the easy part though; the most daunting challenge ahead of me was wearing them in public. So, when I returned to the beach the next day with some Brazilian friends, I already had my Speedo on underneath my shorts. I was ready! After we'd selected a place to laze away the afternoon I put down my bag and slowly slid off my shorts.

At first I felt pretty naked standing there with the light sea breeze touching up against my exposed inner thighs. I won't lie to you, for a few minutes I even felt a little indecent. But just like that I looked like any other *sunga* wearer on the beach, and just like that I didn't feel nearly as conscious as I was expecting to. But thinking about it: what did I really think would happen?

Did I actually imagine a beach full of people would stop what they were doing to look over, point and stare at me? Was I really expecting a conga line of guys in their Speedos to dance around me in celebration that I was now one of them, all against the backdrop of a marching band and fireworks? Well, of course, none of these things happened. In fact, nobody so much as batted an eyelid as I stepped out of my board shorts (and my comfort zone). On reflection, wearing a Speedo wasn't nearly as big a deal to anybody else there except me.

As a Brit, having wet Bermudas clinging uncomfortably to my body after swimming in the sea was just something I considered to be a part of the beach experience. So too was the chafing that came with them. But as I left the beach I thought about how surprisingly comfortable I'd found my new Speedos. I have no intention of taking them back home to the

UK with me, but doing as the Brazilians do on the beach wasn't nearly as bad as I'd expected!

Yet as a guy I can imagine my worries about wearing a Speedo pale in comparison to how some foreign women feel about slipping into the notoriously small Brazilian bikini.

Brazilian Bikinis vs. Western Bikinis

A few years ago I'd taken a trip to the beach with my Brazilian friends and another friend from the UK. After almost an hour of sunbathing in the summer heat, this friend told me that she was going to take a dip in the sea to cool down. As soon as she was out of earshot my friend Carlos quickly sat up in his reclining chair, looked at me and asked quite urgently: "Why is your friend wearing *that* bikini?"

I looked at him like he was about to deliver his punch line, but he continued staring at me very attentively. Perhaps sensing that I was at a bit of a loss for something to say he continued, "Everyone is looking at her; you need to talk to her and tell her she needs to buy a new bikini, a smaller, more Brazilian one."

Now I'm no expert on bikinis, but the one in question looked quite retro to me. Admittedly though, compared to the other bikinis on the beach it had clearly been made with a more generous amount of fabric. My friend is a keen runner with a toned body, and she obviously felt comfortable in what she was wearing. My friend Carlos, however, didn't.

"But this style is quite normal for English people," I argued.

"Andrew, here is Brazil not England. Just tell her to buy a new one!"

Can you even imagine that conversation? "Look, I think we need to go shopping. It's your bikini. It is offensively modest!" Another of our friends (whose tight Lycra was accentuating the recent love affair he'd been having with fast food) had been listening in and confirmed what Carlos was saying. "She should maybe buy a new bikini, Andrew. You should tell her. Women don't wear bikinis this big on the beach in Brazil."

Only here would you be criticized for wearing too much, by someone whose gut is spilling out over his Speedos.

So what is this tiny bikini thing all about? I mean, aren't women over here worried that their bikinis don't tastefully conceal any unsightly bumps like the women I know from back home would? Well, after my first few trips to the beach I became curious and asked a female friend about this.

"I wear mine because it's practical. I know that when I wear it I'm going to get an even tan, it is going to be comfortable and it's also going to be light to walk around in."

I'd never heard of a woman wearing a bikini because of how 'practical' she found it before, so I was convinced that this response was a one off. Believing I hadn't got an answer that was reflective of what most Brazilian women thought, I asked the same question to my other female friends. When they answered that they also found these small bikinis to be 'practical', I became suspicious. It was as if everyone had somehow collectively conspired to hide something from me. I just didn't get it.

"Don't women just wear them because they are inviting you to look at their toned bodies?" I once thought to myself. Well, actually, far from it just being the attractive and toned women on the beach that demand your attention in their small bikinis, there are also many larger women who wear them too. In one of my first blog posts I mentioned how I'd seen an overweight woman in Rio sporting the tiniest of bikinis:

"She emerged from the sea, legs looking like bags of old meat and rolls upon rolls of skin over her bikini bottoms. I was

absolutely mesmerised. She looked like she didn't have a care in the world."

At the time I remember contemplating how I'd expected her to look. Embarrassed? Apologetic? Well, she was neither of these things. Looking back I'm pretty ashamed at myself for thinking like this; she looked at ease with herself on that beach and had every right to wear whatever she felt comfortable in. I guess the one thing that took me by surprise was that she wasn't nearly as self-conscious as I'd expected her to have been.

Nowadays I have come to respect and even admire these women on the beach wearing tiny bikinis, despite having less-than-toned bodies. These ladies seem to be free from the morbid insecurities that affect so many British women. I soon discovered, though, larger women walking around like this aren't a reflection of how all Brazilian women feel about their bodies on the beach. I was once discussing with a student how refreshing it was to see some women wearing practically nothing, despite being overweight. This student responded by pointing out the following:

"Andrew, fat people on the beach in tiny bikinis belong to a certain class of people: the lower classes. Very overweight middle- and upper-class Brazilian women wouldn't dream of going to the beach and walking around like this."

"But what if *you* gained 20 pounds and your friend invited you to the beach?" I asked.

"Well, then I just wouldn't go, or I'd cover up! But I care about what I look like, so my friends and I like to look good on the beach and we work out when we can. We also do our best never to gain weight in the first place."

Then I became incredibly confused. What I was hoping to do was identify one homogeneous Brazilian beach culture, but the deeper I dug the more I had to accept that it was more complicated than this.

Ladies, what I do know to be true, though, is this: those bikini tops must stay on at all times! I had a student once tell me how tacky she thought Kate Middleton was for exposing her breasts on her holiday in France. "She is a princess, Andrew. She shouldn't be going topless. I know this is European culture but exposing your breasts like this is something a Brazilian woman would *never* do!" Hearing this was interesting, because we see pictures of Brazilian women during carnival wearing nothing more than a bit of glitter and strategically placed feathers. But Carnival is Carnival, and outside the confines of the Carnival samba arena (the Sambadrome) you won't really see topless women in public (unless you're on a nudist beach, of course). Not only do Brazilians generally find exposing breasts on the beach tasteless, but it is also downright illegal too!

So there you have it: when it comes to wearing a bikini or Speedo on the beach, if you haven't already done so you might want to suspend any negative prejudgments you have of these garments before coming over here. And if you're able to do this … let me know how! What Brazilians wear to the beach is *still* a mind-boggling source of intrigue for me all these years later, a cultural hangover that I find I'm still trying to shake off every summer. It is also something I really need to get over if I am to successfully integrate myself into Brazilian culture!

Chapter Eleven – Being British In Brazil

I thought I'd do something a little different with this chapter. Instead of giving my interpretation of how I see Brazilian culture, I thought I'd turn the tables and instead write about what Brazilians seem to think of British culture. If you're British and think you can guess what they think about us, make yourself comfortable … you might be in for a bit of a surprise! Some things I've been asked about have been fairly predictable, whilst others have well and truly baffled me. Let me give you a run down on some of these right now, starting with how the Brazilians I've met have responded to the one aspect of our culture that is undeniably British: our love of a good cup of tea.

Tea

"Oh look, it's 5pm," one of my students pointed out as our class started. As if to emphasise his point, he began tapping his finger on the face of his watch.

"Well, yes, it is," I responded after a few seconds of wondering why the time was of such interest to him. I definitely hadn't arrived late for class.

"Yeah, 5 o' clock," he repeated enthusiastically. "It's 5 o' clock."

As soon as he said this he looked at his watch again, which prompted me to look at it too. Then he looked back up at me, so I felt obliged to look at him in the hope he would elaborate on what he was saying. He didn't. And when nothing more was said I started to look at him suspiciously.

Perhaps sensing that this conversation was becoming awkward, he added, "don't you miss your country right now?"

I was confused by how I was supposed to answer this, but I could see from the look in his eyes he was trying to encourage me to acknowledge something. I felt like an actor in a play who'd forgotten my lines, standing opposite someone willing me to remember them.

"Eeeerm," I began, "well, I don't miss it any more than I did five minutes ago. Why do you ask?"

I was puzzled, and from the look on his face I could see that I wasn't the only one. With his eagerness to communicate whatever was on his mind beginning to wane, he then asked me quite hopefully, "don't people in the UK usually have a cup of tea at 5 o' clock?"

"Erm … no," I said, wondering why in God's name he'd thought this.

Well, as it turns out, since this conversation I've been asked about tea at 5 o' clock on a number of occasions. I still have no idea where it has come from, but I know that many Brazilians believe Brits drink tea at this time. Some people back home will enjoy a brew at 5pm, but it's definitely not a tradition or a custom. People drink tea whenever they want a cup, which can be at any time of the day (especially when someone else offers to make it!).

Timing

Thinking about it now though, maybe this thing with the time has come from Brazilians assuming British people are incredibly punctual. "Oh Andrew, you're here already. You are so British. I forgot you work on British time!" said one of my friends once as he arrived fifteen minutes late to the bar we'd arranged to meet at. I've found that being punctual can be a source of amusement for my Brazilian friends.

I once had a student walk into class ten minutes late and remark gleefully (without even a hint of sarcasm), "Oh look, I'm on time!"

"Well, of course you're not," I felt like saying, "You're 10 minutes late!"

Brazilians are notorious for working on a different concept of time. It's as if they wear watches but don't know how to read them; hence why they're always late.

The first time I heard Brazilians talking about 'British time' I was quite surprised. Back home it's the Germans we usually associate with having great time-keeping, not us Brits. So how we've got this reputation for being masters of punctuality here I'm not quite sure.

Back to Tea Drinking

I've already mentioned the question I've been asked about when we drink tea; now let me tell you about another random question I've been asked on *how* we drink it.

I was giving class in a student's house one afternoon when right in the middle of our lesson my student's mother knocked on the door. To my delight she came in holding a tray that had a cup of Earl Grey tea and a plate of biscuits on it. Amazing! I did everything in my power not to bear hug the life out of this woman in appreciation. A brew was exactly what I needed at this moment.

"Thank you so much," I said politely as I looked down at the generous treats on offer. However, noticing that there was no milk in my tea I asked her if it would be OK to have a little to go with it.

My student's mother only started to veil her surprise at my request midway through my question, "Erm, so you would like some, some milk?" She looked over at her daughter distrustfully, as if she were complicit in this sick 'milk with tea' joke. "Would you like hot or cold milk in your tea?" she eventually asked, clearly stepping on new hosting ground with this question.

"Cold is fine," I answered quite tenderly, before thinking how strange it was to see someone looking so bewildered at something that I think of as being so normal. After eight years as an expat, moments like this never grow old. But then if my student's mother believed everything she'd heard about foreigners she might have expected me to have asked for hot milk. The reason I suspect this, as I've mentioned previously, is because 'hot' is how many Brazilians assume we enjoy our beer. Whilst I'm on the subject of temperatures, I'll tell you another question I've been asked a lot in Brazil, one related to the weather.

You're Hot Then You're Cold

So São Paulo gets quite cold during the winter months. When I say cold I'm talking about five or ten degrees, which I'm sure is being met with a few eye rolls right now from those reading in countries where it actually gets really cold. Over here though, because the buildings are not prepared for São Paulo's relatively short winter this city can genuinely feel pretty chilly at this time. Despite living here for a while now, every year I somehow manage to successfully block from my mind just how cold it gets. Needless to say, winter in São Paulo is not my favourite time of year.

I know this admission will surprise a few of the Brazilians I know, who assume I absolutely love the cold. "You must be used to this cold weather, Andrew," many have told me, "because you're British!"

Once (after having this same conversation for the third time in the space of one morning) I was left wondering, "Do Brazilians actually think that during the summer I'm constantly sleeping in a huge freezer, because as a Brit my body genetically needs the cold?" Well, true, I seem to be able to tolerate it better than some Brazilians do, but I'm not 'used to the cold' of the UK anymore. Besides, there I survived the winter months by wearing a lot of clothes, sitting by radiators and drinking plenty of tea. I didn't survive it because my skin is able to adapt to cold weather, like I'm some sort of X Man!

What Do Brits Sound Like To Brazilians?

And then there is my British accent, which I've found has inspired a range of responses, both positive and negative. I was once a few beers into a street party when one of my friends introduced me to a friend of hers. She'd done this in English, so naturally I didn't think twice about continuing the conversation in the same language. However, as soon as I started talking over the music I noticed this girl was shaking her head at me. "I'm sorry," she interrupted, "You are British, aren't you? I studied American English so maybe this is why I can't understand you."

I gave her a reassuring smile and was about to repeat myself, only this time a little slower. But she interrupted me again with a huge smirk on her face. "I think I don't understand you because you sound like you have a hot potato stuck in your mouth."

I looked at this girl for a good few seconds as I tried to process what she'd just said.

"A what?" I asked faintly, with my polite smile now slowly fading. I was unsure if I'd just been insulted or had simply misunderstood what she'd said.

Turns out, I hadn't misunderstood at all!

"I said you sound like you have a hot potato stuck in your mouth. You need to open your mouth a little more when you talk because I can't understand you!"

"Surely she isn't talking about my delightful accent?" I remember thinking at the time. But she really was. I'm not often lost for words, but, I mean, what is the polite way to respond to someone saying this to you? And then I remember wondering just how it's even possible for someone to talk like they have a hot potato *stuck* in their mouth.

Well, as if she could read my mind, this girl fed my curiosity by simulating what someone would look and sound like in this unfortunate situation. She mimicked my British accent with this imaginary hot potato playing heavily around her mouth and her cheeks inflated grotesquely. As far as first impressions go, this girl had exceeded in making a truly awful one on me. It was clear that we were never destined to become BFFs, so I made my excuses and rejoined my American friend (the same friend who has no problem understanding me, most of the time!).

I should point out that this was definitely the most extreme experience I've had of someone reacting negatively to my accent. I do occasionally meet Brazilian English speakers who are so accustomed to American English that my accent proves to be very challenging for them. Having said this, British English is certainly not frowned upon over in São Paulo. One of the most popular chains of English schools here, Cultura Inglesa, is a school that focuses on the teaching of British English.

From my own personal experience too, I've had a lot of students specifically ask for classes with me because of their desire to be exposed to my accent. And, get this, a number of people have even said that they find my accent beautiful to listen to. I genuinely thought I was being mocked the first time I heard a student say this. You see, my northern-English farmer's drawl isn't met with nearly the same level of enthusiasm within the UK as it is by some here.

Back at home, because the Yorkshire accent is quite slow in comparison to other regional accents, I've been told that it makes us sound slightly uneducated (actually, I might have made up that part about people using the word 'slightly'). However, over in Brazil I've had people describe my accent as charming, slow enough for them to understand and even (my favourite) sophisticated.

Brits in Brazilian Culture

There are a few British celebrities who have proved quite popular over here. Randomly one of these includes Jo Frost (aka *Supernanny*, remember her?) who was a dominant fixture of TV schedules a few years ago and a firm favourite of my friend Carlos' Mama. Jamie Oliver and Nigella Lawson are also pretty popular here, too. Oliver's books are a continued presence in Brazilian book shops, and after Nigella's visit to São Paulo in 2013 she managed to cement her popularity with the female housewives I teach by praising the nation's beloved *coxinha* (a food I highly recommend).

Interestingly whilst the chef Gordon Ramsay might be a big deal over in the States and in his native UK, he has yet to leave as big a mark on the Brazilian consciousness as his British rivals have. And whilst I'm on the subject of popular Brits in Brazil, it would be strange of me not to mention the UK's music scene. I've found that British music is one aspect of our culture that is frequently met with a great deal of enthusiasm in Brazil. From The Beatles to Amy Winehouse, Elton John to the Stones, Led Zeppelin to Bowie, Queen to The Sex Pistols, George Michael to Adele, Black Sabbath to erm … One Direction, British music seems to have really resonated with a lot of the Brazilians I've come into contact with.

This may, or may not, be down to these artists being able to really open their mouths wide enough for that potato not to cause any problems when they sing!

Chapter Twelve – Conclusion

For as long as I've been in Brazil, its culture has been a constant source of fascination and intrigue for me. After immersing myself into Brazilian life for about four years, I feel like I have a decent grasp of what to expect from it. Yet, having said this there are a few elements of it that I suspect will forever be lost on me.

The first one? The way Brazilians gush over one meal in particular: rice and beans. They seem to enjoy this dish a whole lot more than I'd ever imagined was humanly possible. Given that you can find some delicious culinary delights in the country (like the *coxinha*, *pastel* and *pão de queijo*), I genuinely don't understand why so many hold rice and beans in such high regard. I mean, it's just rice and beans, right? Well, if you say this to your average Brazilian, this comment may well be met with a look of utter revulsion! They take this meal *very* seriously, after all! And I once had a student tell me that when he visited the UK he found British cuisine 'bland and tasteless'. Then in the same breath he went on to tell me that the longer he was there, the more he missed his rice and beans!

Another thing I haven't really been able to get used to is the way Brazilians greet each other. Yes, I appreciate how cold our handshake is in comparison to a loving hug and/or a couple of theatrical air kisses. Yet on those days when I'm sweating under the intense summer sun, the last thing I want to do is physically go near anyone. I can see from the faces of the women who force themselves to greet me that they're not mad-keen on the idea of getting close to my sweaty body either!

And I don't really understand those Brazilians who step onto the metro in the middle of a phone call, then argue, gesture and shout their way down their handsets. I often wonder how they can be so oblivious to everyone else on the train being able to hear them. Some of these guys actually exude so much passion for whatever it is they're talking about, you could easily be forgiven for thinking they're reciting lines from a Shakespearean tragedy!

Studying Portuguese

One way in which Brazilian culture has become more accessible to me is through studying the language. I'm not going to claim I've become a formidable Portuguese speaker in the last four years, because I really haven't. Actually, it's quite common for my Brazilian friends to screw their faces up when I try to explain something complicated to them in Portuguese, then ask me what the hell I was just talking about! I have some way to go before becoming fluent, but I'll get there … eventually!

In hindsight, I really should have started studying the language from the moment I got here. But as I mentioned earlier, I wasn't keen on learning another language after all those years I'd invested in Japanese. I discovered that I was able to get by quite easily on the basic Portuguese I'd picked up too. Not only this, but the Brazilian friends I made were keen to practise their English on me, my job was teaching English and I also found navigating my way around the city to be pretty straightforward. So life here wasn't all that difficult without knowing much of the lingo, but this meant I became lazy. There were two things that happened about ten months into my stay here though, that gave me the all important kick up the backside I needed to open those language books.

Incident #1

One Tuesday afternoon I went into my local barber shop and noticed that the guy who usually cut my hair wasn't around. I was about to walk out again, but then I noticed an elderly barber sat by the entrance, staring at me from his seat. As soon as we made eye contact he asked me something in Portuguese that I really didn't understand. Not that this mattered; he was already stood up and gesturing for me to sit on his chair.

I'm not particularly bothered about who cuts my hair; unfortunately, I don't really have enough of it to get precious about the quality of the cut. I only ever ask for a 'short, back and sides' anyway, nothing as complicated as a pre-2011 Bieber. So I shrugged my shoulders, sat down and then said the word *curto* (short) quite hopefully to him.

It became clear very early on that this barber was one hell of a conversationalist. Almost as soon as my ass hit that cushioned chair, he began asking me things that were outside the realms of my survival Portuguese. I repeatedly told him I didn't understand, but bizarrely this only encouraged him to ask me more. Now, most people would've given up after a few minutes of having their questions being met with a look of pure confusion, but not this guy! No! This guy was adamant he could tease the answers he wanted out of me through excessive perseverance. To his credit, I was able to answer a few of the questions he'd thrown my way. Yet the more I understood, the more carried away he was getting and this meant the less he was focusing on my haircut.

I remember looking at him in the mirror (if I recall correctly, it was around the same time he was asking me something about The Beatles) and saw that he was opening and closing his scissors in the air mechanically whilst looking intensely at me. Then the unthinkable happened. He brought his scissors close to my head and cut into my ear.

Had he not already been halfway through, and had I not had a class to teach just an hour later, I'd have been out of the barbers shop ASAP. But after accepting his apologies I decided to wait it out and let him finish. The next ten minutes were pretty uncomfortable for both of us. I occasionally dabbed at the blood trickling from my ear with the towel he'd given me, and winced every time he got close with his scissors. The only positive in all of this was that from this moment on, he stopped talking. (He never did get to find out if I knew Paul McCartney personally!)

To my surprise, when he finished trimming my locks he pointed to a cashier in the corner of the room, then he instructed me to go over and pay her. I couldn't believe it! I shook my head, looked quite menacingly at him and then walked out of there. On reflection this was quite brave of me, given that I knew what he was capable of doing with his scissors! "If only I spoke a decent level of Portuguese," I remember thinking to myself, "I could've told Mr. Scissorhands where to stick his payment!"

Incident #2

One afternoon during my first year in São Paulo I was at home watching MTV. I took an instant liking to a song that was playing on the Top 10 countdown by the Brazilian singer Thiago Petit. This prompted me to turn on my laptop and join his Facebook page. A few months later Thiago posted details of an intimate concert he would be performing at the MTV studios later that week. The first 20 people to send their email address to him would get two tickets for this gig. Well, I was the seventh to post mine, guaranteeing me a pair of tickets (and a few months worth of spam from a Russian dating website!).

Days later I was sitting with my flat mate on the floor of a tiny studio, waiting for the concert to start. I'd naively assumed this gig would involve Thiago standing in the middle of the room crooning to us all, and that as an audience member my participation would be limited to applauding the end of each song. Well, yet again, I was wrong!

I was absolutely horrified when an MTV presenter arrived and began to interview people at random, edging ever closer to where I was sitting. I really feared he'd ask me something and expose my awful Portuguese on national TV. I've never felt as relieved as I did the moment he walked past me to interview an excitable woman a few feet away (I'm sure this woman got her dates mixed up and was actually expecting Justin Bieber to show up. She looked *far* too excited to have been there just to see this singer!). Between each song Thiago would make small talk with us all, which usually made everyone laugh. Despite having absolutely *no* idea what this crowd was laughing at, I found myself laughing along with them too. After the show finished I conceded that had I known more Portuguese, I would've felt a lot more comfortable in there.

When the MTV special aired, I saw that a close up of my fake laugh (and scabby ear) had made the final cut; I was relieved that I'd looked like I understood the jokes. But I knew that it was time for me to be able to do more than this; the time had come for me to pull my finger out and get studying.

From left to right: Me, Thiago Petit and Carlos, outside the MTV studios

Three years on and I'm happy I did. Now that I'm able to converse with Brazilians in Portuguese, I have great friends who don't speak a word of English (all of whom are very keen to teach me the most exquisitely offensive words they know!). I also get immense pleasure from being able to haggle down prices of things in Portuguese too. On a number of occasions when I've been at the beach in Rio, I've heard vendors shouting that their cans of beer are five reals. Then they've walked over to me, taken one look at my Casper-like complexion and naturally assumed I don't speak a word of Portuguese. This is when these guys have tried to charge me eight. (This practice of overcharging because someone is assumed to be a non-Brazilian is known here as 'Gringo-tax'.) When you're as tight-fisted as I am, there is truly no greater feeling in the world than being able to assert, quite smugly, that you've already heard the original price and will be paying five reals like everyone else – thank you very much!

As I'm reflecting on my time in Brazil, I'm reminded of the moment that I became aware of how comfortable I'd become here. After about three years here I was watching the sunset with some friends at Praça Pôr do Sol. In front of me were young guys performing *capoeira*, behind me an elderly woman was selling her beer, and to the left of me an amorous couple were kissing (passionately, of course!). As the sun began to dip behind the skyscrapers that dominate the city's horizon, an array of enchanting colours were thrown up into the evening sky. "Wow, how beautiful," I said to my friend, who nodded in agreement.

I then considered how I would have interpreted this same sunset very differently just a few years earlier. Where before I found São Paulo to be ugly, intimidating and bland; I was now looking at it through a different pair of eyes. I hadn't wanted to visit the city initially because it wasn't the Brazil I'd wanted to buy into. However, in allowing myself to see São Paulo for what it is and not how I'd wanted it to be, I've come to accept it on its own terms. In doing so I've grown to appreciate that the true beauty of Brazil lies not just in its spectacular landscapes that attract so many tourists, but also in its people and its very, very unique culture.

About The Author

Andrew Creelman is the author of *Brazil: Life after the Honeymoon Period, The Top 85 Mistakes Brazilians Make in English* and *100 More Mistakes Brazilians Make in English*.

The story continued…

"Do you want to die?" The thief screamed. "Do you want to die?" He repeated, and as Andrew stared down the barrel of the gun, time slowed down, the air around him became still, and he was no longer aware of anything else happening around him. This was when the severity of what could happen in the next few seconds really hit home. He'd managed to avoid being robbed for a number of years, but not this time.

Brazil: Life after the Honeymoon Period is a memoir about Andrew's life as a foreigner living in Brazil. He arrived here when the country's economy was the darling of the developing world and was strong enough to elevate millions into the middle classes. But times were changing, inflation was rising, and a recession was looming. If you've ever wondered what it is like to live in a country in the midst of mass nationwide protests, this is the book for you.

Of course, life here over the last few years wasn't always so intense. Within the book, a number of other questions are also addressed, such as: What was it like to be in the country during the World Cup? What happened at the biggest gay pride parade in the world? Who is this intriguing celebrity - famous simply for having an ass shaped like a watermelon? How possible is it to work as a teacher in Brazil during an economic downturn? And how the hell did Andrew unexpectedly end up being linked, by the world's media, to São Paulo's Osama Bin Laden bar?

Where his first memoir *Trying to Understand Brazilian Culture* was an interpretation of Brazilian culture from a very naïve and unprepared perspective, this follow-up is an exploration of life in the country through a more familiar set of eyes.

Times were changing, and things were about to get very interesting…in more ways than one.

Sample Chapter- The Unwritten Rules for Brazilian House Parties

You'd think that the rules for house parties over here wouldn't differ too much from the rules we stick to in the UK, right? Well, there are a couple of differences that I'd like to share.

My Mariah Carey moment

When my friend turned thirty last year his parents celebrated by throwing a party in their apartment. After accepting the invitation I wanted to double check two things before the big day; the first, what was I supposed to bring? The second, what did "the party starts at eight" really mean? I didn't know if the rules for when to arrive at house parties differed when they were thrown by friend's parents.

"We will have a lot of beer here so you don't need to bring anything," I was told. "And 'the party starts at eight' means arrive sometime after eight." So on the day of the party, I arrived at eight thirty.

As soon as I stepped through the front door, I was introduced to my friend's family. After exchanging pleasantries, I sat down next to a friend who told me he'd arrived just minutes before me. He said that he was happy I'd turned up 'early' too!"

"Andrew, let me get you a beer," said my friend's father. These words fell very kindly on my ears because it was summer, I had perspiration incontinence, and I really needed to cool down. Like seriously, I looked like I'd taken a shower fully clothed before walking into my friend's place (I kind of wish I was exaggerating right now).

So I was handed a beer, and I started to catch up with my friend. Fifteen minutes later, he told me he was going to use the bathroom. At this point, I'd already drunk everything in my can and was really looking forward to beer number two.

So I put my empty can down on the table beside me and waited to find the right moment to ask my friend's parents if I could have another. If I remember correctly, the mother was telling a story at the time. She smiled at me as I caught her eye and then included me in the conversation she was having about one of her work colleagues. I smiled at her for the duration of this incredibly long conversation, hoping that she'd realise I was done with my beer and then offer me another can. However, this story didn't seem to have an end. I didn't really want to interrupt her to ask for another beer because she looked so engrossed in what she was saying.

Then when my friend returned, he had a full can of beer.

"Where did you get that from?" I asked, with false innocence and surprise. Obviously, I knew he hadn't found it down the back of the sofa or just lying around in the bathroom. But my friend's family were all in the living room, and his mum was right in the middle of her story. Or maybe she was still at the beginning, I can't remember. But anyway, she was definitely nowhere near the end! So I knew that he'd not been offered the beer by any member of the family.

"Why do you ask?" my friend smiled as if amused by my ignorance. "I got it from the fridge, of course."

"Well," I began, quietly, so as not to be overheard. "I was waiting for someone to ask me if I would like another beer, I can't believe you've simply helped yourself to a can!"

"Really?" he laughed, "Andrew, you are not Mariah Carey, if you want a beer, maybe you need to move your lazy, gringo body to the fridge and get one!"

I was stunned into silence. The reason I was waiting was not that I was lazy, but because I wouldn't dream of going into someone else's fridge to help myself to a beer, not without their permission anyway. If you did this in England, you probably wouldn't be invited back to another house party!

I hurriedly tried to explain this to my friend, but he wasn't up for believing a word of it. Clearly amused by his own version of events, he interrupted the story my friend's mum was telling about her work colleague. He then announced that I had been waiting to be 'served' a beer.

I was mortified!

"Oh Andrew, no! Just help yourself!" the mum told me. I quickly left the room and headed in the direction of the fridge.

I learnt a valuable lesson that day: When at a party in your friend's family's place, you don't necessarily need to wait to be offered another beer; you can just get one out of the fridge yourself.

Unless it would seem, you really are Mariah Carey!

Are you a Brazilian studying English? Here is the book you should be reading!

The Top 85 Mistakes Brazilians Make in English was written specifically for Brazilians studying English. The author of this book is an experienced native English teacher who has been working in São Paulo for almost five years. During this time he has taught a variety of students, ranging from CEOs of multinational companies to kids, models and journalists, from housewives and actors to a whole host of professionals in between.

It didn't take him too long to realise that the same mistakes were being made by these students again and again...and again! This is when he came up with the idea of writing a book on the common mistakes he hears his Brazilian students making.

Knowing these mistakes is one thing, being able to remember them when speaking English is another. So as well as pointing out common errors, this book also offers some tips and explanations on how to make those mistakes a thing of the past!

You will soon notice that this is definitely not your average English book. It dares to go where the more traditional books don't. As a result you can expect to read about things Brazilians say that are likely to make a native English speaker laugh; those common mistakes that are either going to sound sexual, could embarrass the person you're talking to or are likely to just sound very, very funny!

If your English is of an upper intermediate/advanced level and you are interested in knowing the mistakes your English teacher hears on a daily basis (or those embarrassing mistakes you definitely don't want to be making in meetings with your international colleagues!) The Top 85 Mistakes Brazilians Make in English is the book for you!

So...how many of the 85 mistakes do you make?